Challenge your pupils 3

using problem-solving questions from the
Primary Mathematics Challenge

The Mathematical Association

© The Mathematical Association 2016

All rights reserved.

First published in 2016 by
The Mathematical Association

ISBN 978-0-906588-87-1

Printed and bound in Great Britain: Blissetts, London

Copyright Statement

How to use this book

These problems can be used in several different ways. Here are a few ideas:

1. selected by the teacher for homework, either choosing particular topics or at random
2. extension work in class, selecting problems relating to classwork
3. selecting a problem as a starter for investigative work
4. practice for the papers set in PMC which take place every November (primary schools only).

The problems

Over 200 multiple choice problems from a variety of mathematical topics are provided for use by teachers in primary (and secondary) schools. The aim is to provide interesting mathematical experiences using elementary mathematics topics. Many of the problems can lead to further investigative work.

There are four categories of problems: Easy, Harder, Puzzling and Very Challenging. Most pupils should be able to get the easy problems correct, while the challenging problems will test the brightest young mathematicians in the country!

Answers and Notes

Answers and brief notes are provided for all problems. There are also some ideas for follow up work and extended investigation.

Mathematical Health Warning!

The difficult and challenging problems in this book are difficult! Problems for each pupil should first be selected from the Easy section, and then to progress to the more difficult problems, rather than start with the harder problems. If pupils cannot get a grip on the harder multiple choice problems, they will just guess!

Contents

How to use this book   (i)

Mathematical Health Warning   (i)

Easy problems   1

Harder problems   7

Puzzling problems   17

Very Challenging problems   30

Easy problems – answers and notes   37

Harder problems – answers and notes   43

Puzzling problems – answers and notes   54

Very Challenging problems – answers and notes   69

Easy Problems

E1 What is the value of $1 \times 2 \times 3 \times 4$?

    A 10   B 20   C 24   D 28   E 40

E2 One quarter of a number is 4. What is the number?

    A 16   B 20   C 40   D 64   E 144

E3 Which of the following numbers is not a factor of 50?

    A 5   B 10   C 15   D 25   E 50

E4 Calculate $1 + 2 + 3 + 4 + 5 + 6 + 7 + 8 + 9 + 10$.

    A 55   B 95   C 135   D 145   E 155

E5 Add together one dozen and half a dozen.

    A 3   B 6   C 12   D 18   E 24

E6 If a parrot learns five new words every fifteen minutes, how many new words will it learn in an hour?

    A 5   B 10   C 15   D 20   E 60

E7 In seven years' time, Alacoe will be 13 years old. How old was she last year?

    A 4   B 5   C 6   D 7   E 8

E8 Which of these lengths is the longest?

    A 3.4 m   B 0.34 m   C 34 cm   D 3.4 cm   E 34 mm

E9 An apple a day keeps the doctor away; so how many apples in a week?

    A 1   B 5   C 7   D 8   E 14

E10 A ladybird has six legs. Altogether, how many legs do sixty-six ladybirds have?

    A 36   B 66   C 396   D 666   E 3636

Easy Problems

E11 What fraction of this square is shaded black?

A $\dfrac{1}{5}$ B $\dfrac{1}{4}$ C $\dfrac{4}{9}$ D $\dfrac{5}{9}$ E $\dfrac{4}{5}$

E12 In our garage we have five bicycles, three tricycles and one quad bike.
How many wheels are there altogether?

A 3   B 9   C 18   D 23   E 27

E13 Are you in trouble? Calculate 111 + 333 + 555.

A 555   B 666   C 777   D 888   E 999

E14 How many of these numbers are larger than eleven thousand?

1104   9999   10 999   21 000   100 014

A None   B 1   C 2   D 3   E 4

E15 I need a lot of toys. Which of these offers give me the cheapest price for each toy?

A buy 1, get 1 free   B buy 2, get 2 free   C buy 3, get 3 free
D buy 4, get 4 free   E there's no difference – they are all the same

E16 Penny Lane School raised 53 000 pennies for charity.
How much is this worth?

A £53   B £530   C £5300   D £53000   E £530 000

E17 I have 30 counters; some are red and the rest are blue. There are twice as many red counters as there are blue counters.
How many red counters are there?

A 2   B 10   C 15   D 20   E 24

E18 A number has factors 2, 3 and 5. What is the smallest it can be?

A 10   B 15   C 30   D 45   E 60

Easy Problems

E19

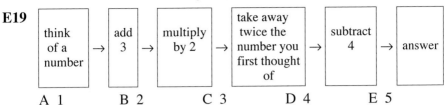

| think of a number | → | add 3 | → | multiply by 2 | → | take away twice the number you first thought of | → | subtract 4 | → | answer |

A 1 B 2 C 3 D 4 E 5

E20 I am thinking of a prime number less than twenty. When I reverse its digits, I get the same number. What is the number?

A 7 B 11 C 13 D 17 E 19

E21 How much does Party Patty pay when she orders ten pepperoni pizzas costing 5.99 each?

A £50 B £590 C £59.90 D £59.99 E £599

E22 For one journey my bus fare has increased from £2.05 to £2.15. I travel this journey twice each day of the week from Monday to Friday. How much *extra* do I pay in one week?

A 10p B 50p C £1 D £10.75 E £21.50

E23 On *The Z Factor* (a mathematical talent show) a meter measures the amount of applause. What applause rating does the arrow indicate?

A 8.5 B 8.95 C 8.99 D 9.1 E 9.5

E24 In a piece of music, a note like ♩ is worth one beat (of time); ♪ is worth half a beat; 𝅗𝅥 is worth 2 beats and 𝅝 is worth 4 beats.

How many beats does this piece of music add up to?

A 4 B 5 C 6 D 7 E 8

Easy Problems

E25 Bert starts his homework at 5.15 pm and finishes it at
6.05 pm.
During this time he has a break of 10 minutes.
How long does he spend working on his homework?

A 35 min   B 40 min   C 45 min   D 50 min   E 1 hr

E26 On a very cold day last winter, the thermometer read
−8°C. The next day the temperature had fallen by 8
degrees. What was the new temperature?

A −16°C   B −8°C   C 0°C
D 8°C   E 88°C

E27 Which of these statements is correct?

A 3 > 4   B 3 ⩾ 4   C 4 < 3   D 4 ⩽ 3   E 4 > 3

E28 What is the name of the shape used to make the head
of this bird?

A circle   B ellipse   C rectangle   D trapezium E triangle

E29 Patti is making a patio using square slabs. She has
started the patio (see the diagram), but she wants it to
be twice as long and twice as wide.
How many slabs will she need altogether?

A 6   B 8   C 10   D 16   E 32

E30 Each of an equilateral triangle, a square, a regular pentagon and a
regular hexagon has a perimeter of 60cm. Which of these shapes has
the largest side length?

A hexagon   B pentagon   C square
D triangle   E they are all the same

E31 Which of the following shapes is not an octagon?

A ◯   B ⬡   C ⌓   D ⬡   E ◁

4

Easy Problems

E32 Every single letter in one of these words has mirror symmetry. Which word is it?

A ADDITION   B ANGLE   C SQUARE
D RULER   E CUBE

E33 I cut a regular pentagon into two pieces with a straight cut. Which of these is it impossible to obtain?

A 1 triangle and 1 hexagon B 2 quadrilaterals   C 1
triangle and 1 quadrilateral D 1 triangle and 1 pentagon
E 2 triangles

E34 I have a paper rectangle. If I make one fold by putting one corner exactly over its diagonally opposite corner, what outline shape do I get?

A ▭   B ◯   C △   D ▱   E ⬠

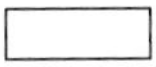

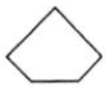

E35 The shape shown here is made of two cuboids.
What is the length marked *x*?

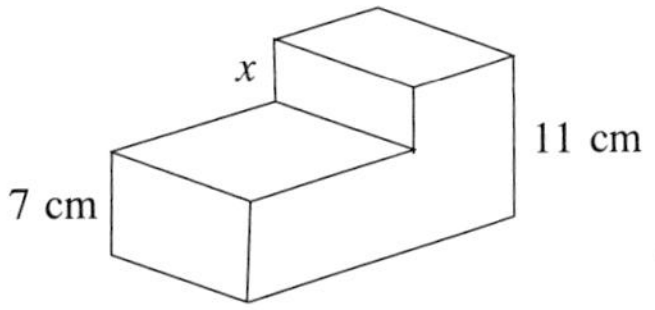

7 cm   *x*   11 cm

A 3.5 cm   B 4 cm   C 4.5 cm   D 5 cm   E 5.5 cm

E36 Baby Finn is building a cube from individual smaller cube bricks.
How many more bricks does he need to make a 3 × 3 × 3 cube?

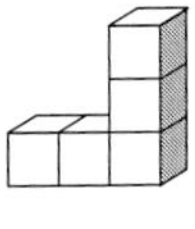

A 4   B 10   C 16   D 22   E 28

E37 On the right the mouse has been rotated and then reflected. Which of the following would show how the polecat would become if it were rotated and then reflected in the same way?

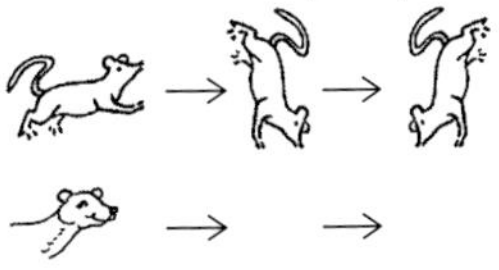

A    B    C    D    E

Easy Problems

E38 How many of these five shapes have <u>exactly</u> one line of symmetry?

A 1   B 2   C 3   D 4   E 5

E39 I throw four normal six-sided dice. What is the highest total I can expect to get?

A 4   B 8   C 14   D 23   E 24

E40 How many rectangles of different sizes can be seen here?

A 2   B 3   C 4   D 5   E 6

E41 How many different letters are there is the phrase PRIMARY MATHEMATICS CHALLENGE?

A 12   B 14   C 16   D 18   E 20

E42 What is the word that is best to describe the probability that you could eat a thousand hard boiled eggs in one minute?

A impossible   B unlikely   C possible
D likely   E certain

E43 I must use three colours (red, white and blue) in the badge shown. How many different badges can I make with the three colours?

A 3   B 4   C 5   D 6   E 9

E44 My music teacher Miss Quaver was happily walking across the playground when a bird flew past. What word best describes the probability of her being hit on the head by a bird dropping?

A impossible   B very unlikely   C evens
D very likely   E certain

Harder Problems

H1   Which of the following decimal fractions has the smallest value?

(A) 0.00001   B 0.0001   C 0.001   D 0.01   E 0.1

H2   At Hugh Deeney School, 1200 children escaped from the playground. At each junction down the road, half went right and half went left. How many children went towards the police station?

A 150   B 241   (C) 300   D 400   E 600

H3   February 2014 has 28 days. Which the following calculations is true?

A $2 \times 0 \times 14 = 28$ B $2 + 0 \times 14 = 28$ (C) $(2 + 0) \times 14 = 28$
D $2 + 0 + 14 = 28$ E $2 \times 0 + 14 = 28$

H4   Willy Sneeze has to take 7.5ml of Yucky medicine four times a day. How many days will a 300ml bottle last him?

A 4   B $7\frac{1}{2}$ (C) 10   D 30   E 40

H5   If a machine stitches a head onto 150 toy bears every 5 minutes, how many heads will it stitch on in 30 seconds?

A 5   B 10   (C) 15   D 20   E 25

H6   A bouncy ball is dropped from a height of 160 cm. It bounces twice and each time reaches three-quarters of its previous height.
How high does it rise on the second bounce?

A 80 cm   (B) 90 cm   C 99 cm   D 108 cm   E 120 cm

H7   In 2011, a quarter of a million DVDs of *Doctor Why* were sold.
In 2012, the number of sales increased by 10%.
How many people bought a *Doctor Why* DVD in 2012?

A 25 000   B 27 500   C 250 000   (D) 275 000   E 2 750 000

Harder Problems

H8 In Hampstead, a suburb of north London, it costs 20p to park a car for 7 ½ minutes.
If I leave my car there for 1 hour how much must I pay?

    A 90p   B £1.60   C £2.00   D £2.40   E £3.00

H9 Costa Packet pays 90p for a coffee in her local coffee bar. If she buys five cups of coffee she gets one extra cup free, so how much does she effectively pay for each cup of coffee?

    A 15p   B 75p   C 90p   D £4.50   E £5.40

H10 What is the nearest number to 200 which is exactly divisible by 17?

    A 187   B 197   C 203   D 204   E 221

H11 Pavel thinks of a prime number greater than 10. Which of the following cannot be the units digit for this prime number?

    A 1   B 3   C 5   D 7   E 9

H12 Two positive numbers have a product of 90 and a difference of 9. What is their sum?

    A 19   B 21   C 23   D 25   E 33

H13 Which of these is not a factor of 2012?

    A 2   B 4   C 8   D 503   E 1006

H14 Sue has 3 horses who each drink 9 gallons of water a day. When the taps froze in their field, she had to drive to them, taking their water in 4-gallon containers. She only has 3 of these. How many trips in her car did she have to make each day?

    A 1   B 2   C 3   D 4   E 5

[Handwritten annotations: "didn't Understand the question", "27 gallons", "if you don't understand, Start with basic question"]

Harder Problems

H15 Marcus Absent goes to school from Monday to Friday only when there is an 's' in the name of the day. During the 13 weeks of last term, how many days did he go to school?

    A 3   B 13   C 16   (D 39)   E 65

H16 I think of a number, double it, subtract 4 and then halve it. I end up with 8. What number did I start with?

    A 2   B 8   (C 10)   D 16   E 28

H17 Jack is 3 years older than Jill. The sum of their ages is 25. What is the product of their ages?

    A 25   B 144   C 150 (D 154)   E it's impossible to say

H18 The River Nile in Africa is 6650 km long, whereas the Roe River in Montana, USA is a mere 61 m. Approximately how many times longer is the Nile than the Roe?

    A 1 000 000 (B 100 000)   C 10 000   D 1000   E 100

H19 Which of the following is a square AND a cube number?

    A 4   B 8   C 9   D 27   (E 64)

H20 Milly is 6, Molly is 8, Mommy is 38 and Daddy is 36. In how many years' time will their ages total 100?

    A 2   (B 3)   C 4   D 5   E 6

(H21) Polly Bagg lives in a small town of 500 people. Every day each person gets one polythene bag from the local shop. If all the people in the town decided to use their own bags instead, roughly how many bags would be saved in a year?

confused

    A 500 million   B 1800   C 18 000 (D 180 000) E 1.8

500×365 = 180,000

Harder Problems

H22 Robyn Hoodie must share out the money with the poor, but is allowed to keep any left over change. What gives Robyn the most left over change?

A £2 ÷ 3   B £3 ÷ 4   C £4 ÷ 5   D £5 ÷ 6   E £6 ÷ 7

H23 Suppose we live in a world in which children can have negative amounts of money in their pocket. Dolores starts with £1, spends £1.30, and then finds 75p?
How much will Delores have now?

A −45p   B 0p   C 45p   D 75p   E £2.05

H24 What is thirteen thousand added to thirteen hundred and thirteen?

A 13 113   B 13 413   C 14 313   D 131 313   E 1 301 313

H25 In the year 2012, the first 'Friday the Thirteenth' fell in January. When will the next 'Friday the Thirteenth' fall?

A February   B March   C April
              D May   E June

H26 On a train journey we left Edinburgh at 10.30 and arrived at (King's Cross) London at 14.50. The train stopped at only Newcastle, Darlington and York, for 5 minutes each time. For how minutes was the train moving on this journey?

A 240   B 245   C 260   D 405   E 420

H27 My local shop will make photocopies either for 10p per photocopy if I make fewer than 50 copies or for 7p per photocopy if I make 50 copies or more. I want to make 45 copies.
How much would I save by making 50 copies instead?

A 70p   B 90p   C £1   D £1.20   E £1.30

H28 The time on the clock is 11 o'clock. What is the size of the smaller angle (in degrees) between the hour and the minute hand on the clock?

A 15   B 30   C 45   D 48   E 330

10

Harder Problems

H29 A train leaves Eltham station at 10.37, arriving at London Bridge at 11.05. On the way it stops at 4 stations, spending an average of 45 seconds at each station. For how many minutes between Eltham and London Bridge is it actually moving?

    A 21   B 22   C 25   D 28   E 31

H30 My name is Speedy. It takes me 3 minutes to cycle to school, which is half a mile away from my home. What is my average cycling speed?

    A 4 mph   B 6 mph   C 8 mph   D 10 mph   E 12 mph

H31 The Olympic Velodrome has a 250 m track. How many circuits does a cyclist have to do to complete a 30 km race?

    A 4   B 12   C 30   D 40   E 120

1st Nov
1-28 (29 Nov)

H32 Given that 1st November 2010 was a Monday, on what day did 1st December fall that year?

Unsure

    A Monday   B Tuesday   C Wednesday
    D Saturday   E Sunday

H33 The dates below are for the reigns of five English kings. Which of these five kings was king for the longest time?

    A Henry I B Henry II C Henry III D Henry IV E Henry V
      1100   1154   1216   1399   1413
     –1136   –1189   –1272   –1413   –1422

H34 If # + # + 15 = 5 × #, then what does # equal?   ← skipped!!

    A 3   B 4   C 5   D 6   E 7

H35 Which of the numbers below makes its square when you multiply its value by the number of letters in its name?

confused

    A 2   B 3   C 4   D 6   E 7

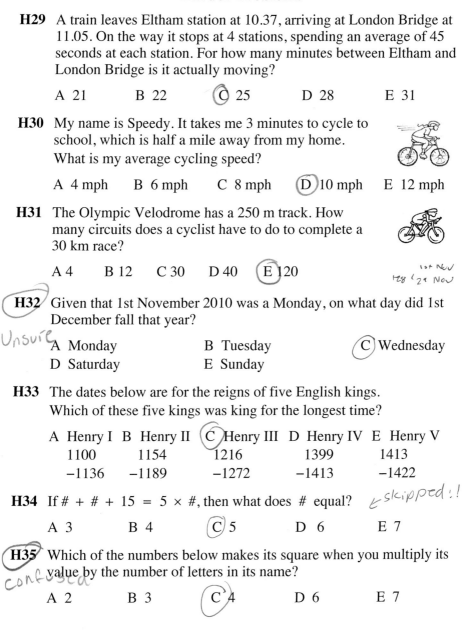

Harder Problems

H36 The dotted lines are vertical and the other lines are all parallel.

Which formula calculates the length of the line marked x?

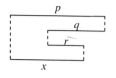

A $p - q - r$ B $p - q + r$ C $p + q - r$

D $p + q + r$ E $q + r - p$

H37 In his garden, Mick Sterbes has a pathway of square stones, each 1 m wide. He painted out a route for his pet snail Herbert, starting at the centre of one of the stones, and going through at the centres of all the other stones. How long is his route?

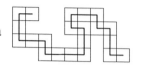

A 19 m   B 20 m   C 21 m   D 22 m   E 23 m

H38 Which of these solids has the most edges?

A tetrahedron   B cube   C square-based pyramid

D hexagonal prism   E octahedron

H39 How many pairs of parallel faces are there on a cube?

A 1   B 2   C 3   D 4   E 5

H40 June 1st 2013 falls on a Saturday. On what day will July 1st 2013 fall? Unsure

A Monday   B Wednesday   C Friday

D Saturday   E Sunday

H41 Stryka Lite is playing with matches. Stryka fits together five matches to make a pentagon. How many more matches does Stryka need to make a pentagonal pyramid?

A 5   B 10   C 15   D 20   E 25

Harder Problems

H42 *confused* In 2011 the police asked five schoolgirls for their dates of birth. Which of them did not tell a lie?

A Neoprene (17.13.2001)　　　B Nylon (32.05.2000)

C Formica (14.07.2012)　　　D Teflon (16.08.2001)

E Trogamid (30.02.2002)

H43 My teacher Mr Oak says "That's great" half the time, "That's bad" a quarter of the time, "That's cool" an eighth of the time and "Solid" the rest of the time. What fraction of the time does he say "Solid"?

A $\frac{1}{8}$　　　B $\frac{1}{6}$　　　C $\frac{1}{4}$　　　D $\frac{1}{3}$　　　E $\frac{1}{2}$

H44 It takes Sennet the centipede 8 seconds to put on a sock and 12 seconds to put on a shoe. She can only do one thing at a time.

How long will it take Sennet to put socks and shoes on all her 100 legs?

A 200 seconds　　B 800 seconds　　C 1200 seconds

D 2000 seconds　　E 2000 minutes

H45 The age of my granny is equal to the number of eyes on our goldfish times the number of legs on our dog times the number of tentacles on our octopus plus the number of toes on one of my feet. How old is she?

A 48　　B 56　　C 64　　D 68　　E 69

H46 Owen D. Bank wants to save up for the latest DS game, which costs £15. If he saves £1 the first week, £2 the second week, £4 the third week and continues doubling, how many weeks will it take him to reach his target?

A 2　　　B 4　　　C 6　　　D 12　　　E 15

Harder Problems

H47 *confused* A car, badly designed by a Year 4 pupil, has square wheels with sides 25 cm long. How many times will the wheels of this car turn right round if it travels 1 km without any slipping?

A 1000   B 2000   C 4000   D 10 000   E 40 000

H48 Hugh Boyd is making a rectangular block out of centimetre cubes. It will measure 4 cm × 3 cm × 5 cm when it is finished. So far Hugh has used up 43 cubes. How many more cubes does he need to finish his block?

A 15   B 17   C 27   D 30   E 60

H49 You go into this maze at the arrow. If you move into the neighbouring hexagon according to the direction shown each time, at which point will you come out of the maze?

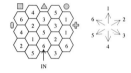

A ◖   B ▣   C △   D ◎   E ✛

H50 I have an isosceles triangle whose perimeter is 30 cm. The longest side of my triangle is 12 cm, so what are the lengths of each of the other two sides?

A 6 cm   B 9 cm   C 10 cm   D 12 cm   E 18 cm

H51 What fraction of this regular hexagon is shaded?

A $\dfrac{1}{4}$ B $\dfrac{1}{3}$ C $\dfrac{1}{2}$ D $\dfrac{2}{3}$ E $\dfrac{3}{4}$

H52 Each of the midpoints of the edges of a square is joined to form a smaller square. The area of the smaller square is 20 cm².

What is the area of the larger square?

A 10 cm²   B 20 cm²   C 40 cm²   D 60 cm²   E 80 cm²

14

Harder Problems

H53 A security camera is placed in the corner of a square room and can detect burglars in the area shaded in the diagram. The two dashed lines from the corner go to the middle of each of the far sides.

What fraction of the area of the room is the shaded area?

A $\frac{1}{4}$　　　B $\frac{3}{8}$　　　(C) $\frac{1}{2}$　　　D $\frac{5}{8}$　　　E $\frac{3}{4}$

H54 I have a box containing 36 chocolates, and a spinner that can stop on four equal areas, each indicating an action.
I spin the spinner 36 times. How many chocolates would I expect to be left in the box?

A 0　　　(B) 9　　　C 18　　　D 27　　　E 36

H55 These five shapes all fit into 2 cm squares, with their sides just touching the squares as shown in the diagram. Which shaded shape has the largest area?

A 　　(B) 　　C 　　D 　　E

H56 Two identical triangles shown here can be picked up, turned and fitted together edge to edge to make new shapes.
Which of these shapes cannot be made?

(A) a rhombus　　　B a rectangle　　　C a triangle
D a kite　　　E a parallelogram

H57 Kate cuts a small triangle from each vertex of a regular hexagon. How many edges does the new shape have?

A 3　　B 6　　C 9　　D 10　　(E) 12

triangle or old hexagon

15

Harder Problems

H58 This shape has been cut from a
3 cm × 3 cm × 3 cm cube.
Four pieces, each 1 cm × 1 cm × 3 cm have
been removed.
What is the volume of the shape?

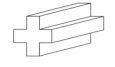

A 9 cm³   B 12 cm³   C 15 cm³   D 23 cm³   E 24 cm³

H59 I am having a bath. I wait for a minute, and then get out. I pull out
the plug, letting the water drain away. Which of the following
graphs best shows the depth of the water in the bath during this
time?

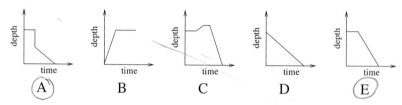

  A   B   C   D   E

H60 On its roof, a police car has a three-digit number
divisible by 7. An albatross dropping has covered
the last digit.
What is the last digit?

A 4 B 5 C 6 D 7 E 8

H61 A sergeant stands too long in the sun and gets
confused. His troops are lined up facing North.
Then he gives the order to "Right Turn" 70 times,
and his troops do so. In which direction are the
troops facing at the end?

A North B East C South D West E West-South-West

16

Puzzling Problems

P1 If you wrote all the numbers from 1 to 99 on a piece of paper, what would the digits add up to?

A 899   B 900   C 910   D 990   E 999

P2 What is the next number in this sequence? 1, 2, 3, 6, 11, 20, 37, ___ ?

A 47   B 54   C 57   D 68   E 74

P3 What the value of : $\dfrac{(3 + 7 + 10) \times (1000 - 8)}{992}$?

A 12   B 20   C 40   D 98   E 100

P4 Bhupinder was born on her granny's 48th birthday. This year Bhupinder noticed that her age, her mother's age and her granny's age were all even square numbers. How old is Bhupinder's mother?

A 25   B 36   C 48   D 49   E 64

P5 In a family with 2 boys and 2 girls, the sum of the children's ages is 42. The 2 boys were born 2 years apart, and so were the girls. The younger boy is twice the age of the older girl. How old is the youngest child? $5 + 7 + 14 + 16 = 42$

A 5   B 6   C 7   D 8   E 9

P6 Isobel is taller than Sarah. Emily is shorter than Isobel, but taller than Sarah. Alice is shorter than Rachel, but taller than both Emily and Isobel. Whose height is the middle for the group?

Rachel
Alice
Isobel
Emily
Sarah

A Alice   B Emily   C Isobel   D Rachel   E Sarah

P7 In the UK Chess Challenge players receive 3 points for a win, 2 for a draw and 1 for a loss. Bill Bishop played 7 games, gaining 16 points. He only drew 1 game, so how many games did he win? $16 - 2 = 14$ 14 points 6 game

A 1   B 2   C 3   D 4   E 5

P8 2011 is a prime number. One of these numbers is also prime. Which one?

A 2012   B 2013   C 2015   D 2017   E 2019

17

Puzzling Problems

P9 Edina Cloud bought 2 cakes and a doughnut for 80p. She then bought 3 cakes and 2 doughnuts for £1.30. How much is one doughnut?

A 10p B 20p C 30p D 50p E 80p

P10 Nerdy Nicky thought it would be a good idea to write the number 2011 over and over again. Several days later, Nicky had written exactly 2011 digits. What were the last four digits to have been written?

A 0112 B 1021 C 1120 D 1201 E 2100

P11 Gurpreet starts reading a book on page 1. She is about to start Chapter 7, which begins on page 49, when her mother calls her down to supper.
What is the average number of pages per chapter in her book so far?

A 6 B 7 C 8 D 10 E 48

P12 How many times faster does the minute hand of a clock go round compared to the hour hand?

A 4 B 6 C 10 D 12 E 60

P13 A car travelling at 30 mph does 48 miles to the gallon and has only half a gallon left.
How many miles will it be before the car runs out of petrol?

A 8 B 12 C 16 D 20 E 24

P14 Alice and her Dad have a total weight of 117 kg. Alice and her Mum weigh 88 kg between them. Mum and Dad together weigh 161 kg. What is the total weight of Mum, Dad and Alice?

A 122 kg B 183 kg C 244 kg D 366 kg E 488 kg

P15 A palindromic number is a number whose digits are the same when read forwards as backwards (for example 2002). In how many years from now (2013) will the year next be a palindromic number?

A 11 B 33 C 99 D 111 E 131

18

Puzzling Problems

P16 In the number for the year 2011, the thousands digit is the sum of the hundreds, tens and units digits. In how many years' time will this happen again?

A 9   B 99   C 101   D 999   E 1001

P17 What is the value of n if $\sqrt{16} + \sqrt{n} = 8$?
(Remember $\sqrt{}$ means square root.)

A 1   B 2   C 4   D 8   E 16

P18 Which of the following cannot be an odd number?

A a prime number   B a multiple of 3
C a square number   D a multiple of 30
E a factor of 3

P19 You probably already know that $2014 = 2 \times 19 \times 53$.
How many factors does 2014 have, other than 1 and 2014 itself?

A 2   B 4   C 5   D 6   E 8

P20 What is the difference between the largest single-digit prime number and the smallest three-digit prime number? $101 - 7 = 94$

A 94   B 95   C 96   D 97   E 98

P21 Which is the next prime number after 2012?

A 2013   B 2014   C 2015   D 2016   E 2017

P22 I am thinking of a prime number less than 20. When I reverse its digits, I get another prime number.
When I multiply these two prime numbers together I get 403. What prime number did I think of?

A 11   B 13   C 17   D 19   E 31

P23 The first and third digits of the five-digit number @6@41 are the same.
If the number is exactly divisible by 9, what digit does @ represent?

A 2   B 4   C 6   D 8   E 9

Puzzling Problems

P24 Salma Nella knows that one of her feet smells more than the other. So she changes her sock on one foot every two days and on the other foot every three days. How many socks does she need to wash after 24 days?

A 10   B 12   C 16   D 20   E 24

P25 Gus and Harry took Ian out to lunch and agreed to share the bill equally. Unfortunately, Ian forgot his wallet, and his friends each had to pay an extra £5 to cover his part of the bill. What was the total bill?

A £10   B £15   C £25   D £30   E £45

P26 Suppose that a doctor in Jabbemall Hospital gets £10 for every 20 flu injections given to patients. At present he can give 2 injections a minute. If he increases his speed to 36 injections per minute, how much could he earn in 20 minutes?

A £20   B £40   C £80   D £200   E £360

P27 Jenny Juice was picking strawberries in a field. When she dropped a bowl of strawberries on ground, one third of them were eaten by wasps, one quarter by ants and one sixth by a maggot.
What fraction of the strawberries was left?

A one third   B one quarter   C one fifth
D one sixth   E one twelfth

P28 One quarter of a bottle of toad juice consists of stewed slime; one quarter of the rest of the bottle consists of melted mud, and that leaves just 90 ml of stagnant sludge. How many millilitres of toad juice are there when the bottle is full?

A 10 ml   B 40 ml   C 70 ml   D 90 ml   E 160 ml

Puzzling Problems

P29 Willy Stockitt likes to display his tins of beans in just one large triangular pile. His shop window is 80 cm high and 42 cm wide, and his bean tins are 10 cm high and 5 cm wide.

What is the largest number of tins he can display in his window? *guessed, need to memorize triangular nums*

A 15   B 21   C 28   D 36   E 45

80
42
160
3200
3360
45
×5
225

P30 My head teacher is buying stickers, each with a single digit on, so that all 100 chairs in the school hall can be numbered. How many stickers with a figure 7 on have to be bought?

A 7   B 10   C 17   D 19   E 20

P31 The school inspector checks the attendance records and discovers that Marcus Absent has only been at school for 80% of the time. If the school year has 190 days, how many school days has he missed? (1 week = 5 school days)

19
× 2
38

A 19 days   B 20 days   C 7 weeks, 3 days
D 19 weeks   E 38 weeks   *didn't they ask class?*

P32 My school has 23 teachers. At today's staff meeting 3 teachers are missing, and a quarter of those present are asleep. Of those that are present and awake, 20% are texting. The rest are listening to the Head. How many are listening to the Head?

A 12   B 13   C 14   D 15   E 0

P33 John was 13 when the 1948 London Olympics took place. How old was he at the time of the London Olympics in July 2012? *64 yrs (unsure which one)*

A $\frac{1}{4}$ of a century −1 year   B 6 decades + 1 year
C 6 decades -1 year   D $\frac{4}{5}$ of a century −3 years
E $\frac{1}{2}$ of a century + 1 year

Puzzling Problems

P34 Tom is at 12 o'clock, and Jerry is at 6 o'clock. At the same time they both start to run clockwise, with Tom running one and a half times as fast as Jerry. At which number on the clock do they first meet?

A 3   B 6   C 9   D 12   E they never meet

P35 One of Hickory Dickory clocks always shows the correct time, and the other loses a minute every ten minutes. If Hickory starts them both at 6 pm, both showing the correct time, what time will the slower clock say when the correct one chimes at 1 am?

A 11.42 pm   B 11.50 pm   C 12.10 am
D 12.18 am   E 12.53 am

P36 Julian is 34 days older than Kylie, and Kylie is 43 days older than Luigi. This year Julian's birthday is on a Wednesday in June. On what day is Luigi's birthday this year?

A Monday   B Tuesday   C Wednesday
D Thursday   E Friday

P37 In an election, only 50% of the citizens voted. Of these, 60% voted for the winning party.
What percentage of the citizens voted for the winning party?

A 30%   B 40%   C 50%   D 60%   E 70%

P38 Mustafa Lok wishes to choose his four-digit padlock code so that it is a multiple of 4 and each digit after the first is one more than the previous digit. What is the code he chooses?

A 1234   B 2468   C 3456   D 4444   E 5678

Puzzling Problems

P39 Miss Ella Stick likes to stretch her able pupils. In proportion to their height, who gets the greatest stretch? *Confused*

A Aled, from 100 cm to 105 cm   B Bertie, from 103 cm to 106 cm
C Carmen, from 120 cm to 125 cm D Daisy, from 125 cm to 128 cm
E Ethan, from 130 cm to 133 cm.

P40 The tops of the seven water fountains in the Italian city of Reggio Emilia form a straight line. The first one rises 120 cm and the last on rises 12 cm.
How high does the third water fountain from the left rise?

A 66 cm   B 72 cm   C 84 cm   D 90 cm   E 102 cm

P41 Four football teams play each of the other three teams once. A win scores 3 points, a draw scores 1 point and a loss scores nothing.
Some figures in the following table are missing, so how many points did the Quads get?

	Play	Win	Draw	Lose	Points
Parallelas	3	3	0	0	9
Quads	3	2	0	1	6
Wrekkies	3	0	1	2	1
Kytes	3	0	1	2	1

A 1   B 4   C 6   D 7   E 10

P42 We are told that $a + b = 6$, $a + b + c = 10$ and $c + d = 6$.
How many of the values of a, b, c and d can we work out?

A 0   B 1   C 2   D 3   E 4

P43 In the diagram, the length of PS is three times the length of SQ. The length of RS is 4 cm and is twice the length of SQ.
What is the area of triangle PQR?

A 12 cm²   B 16 cm²   C 24 cm²   D 30 cm²   E 32 cm²

23

Puzzling Problems

P44 What is the size of the angle marked $x°$ in this diagram?
(The lengths *PS*, *SQ* and *RQ* are all equal.) Confused

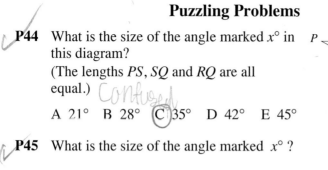

A 21°   B 28°   C 35°   D 42°   E 45°

P45 What is the size of the angle marked $x°$?

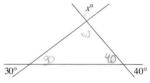

A 30°   B 40°   C 70°
D 110°   E 170°

P46 The angles of a triangle are in the ratio 1 : 2 : 3. What type of triangle is it?

A equilateral   B right-angled isosceles
C right-angled scalene   D isosceles but not right-angled
E scalene but not right-angled

P47 Arky Meedes realises he can calculate the height h of a tower without climbing to the top and using a tape measure.
He notices that when the sun just appears over the top of the tower, the shadow of a 2 m stick is 4 m long.
What is the height of the tower? Confused

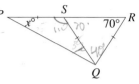

A 16 m   B 18 m   C 32 m   D 36 m   E 64 m

P48 What is the volume of this wedge in cm³?

A 19   B 30   C 90   D 180   E 360

P49 The diagram shows a tessellation of squares and equilateral triangles, which could go on forever. Approximately what percentage of the tessellation is covered with the equilateral triangles?

A 45%   B 55%   C 65%   D 75%   E 85%

24

Puzzling Problems

P50 The diagram shows 3 rectangles piled up, one on top of the other. Each of the smaller rectangles has half of the area of the next.
What fraction of rectangle *ABCD* is unshaded?

A $\dfrac{1}{8}$　B $\dfrac{1}{4}$　C $\dfrac{1}{3}$　D $\dfrac{3}{8}$　E $\dfrac{1}{2}$

P51 The diagram shows regular octagons and squares. What is the size of angle *x*°?

A 108° B 120° C 124° D 132° E 135°

P52 Each of the identical octagons in the diagram is 10 cm high and 10 cm wide and has an area of 64 cm². What is the area of one of the shaded squares?

A 4 cm²　　　B 9 cm²　　　C 16 cm²
D 25 cm²　　　E 36 cm²

P53 Saskia's rose bed measures 3 metres by 1 metre. Amy's rose bed is three times as long, but a third as wide. What is the area of Amy's rose bed?

A 2 m²　B 3 m²　C 3.5 m²　D 4 m²　E 6 m²

P54 The shaded area is a plan for a flower-bed in the shape of a V-shaped hexagon, formed from two overlapping right-angled isosceles triangles.
What is the area of the flower-bed? *confused*

A 4.5 m²　B 8 m²　C 9 m²　D 12.5 m²　E 18 m²

P55 The diagram shows four triangles, each having sides of 3 cm, 4 cm and 5 cm. What is the length of the perimeter of this shape?

A 12 cm　B 20 cm　C 24 cm　D 28 cm　E 48 cm

Puzzling Problems

P56 The volume of the shape in the diagram is 120 cm³. What could the lengths of x and y be, in cm?

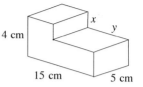

4 cm · 15 cm · 5 cm

A 1, 36   B 2, 18   C 3, 12   D 4, 9   E 6, 6

P57 Alice pours 10 litres of treacle into 25 identical teapots for the Mad Hatter. How much treacle is in each teapot?

A 25 ml   B 40 ml   C 250 ml
D 400 ml   E 500 ml

P58 Here are two water tanks. A water pipe can fill the smaller tank in 20 minutes. How long would it take to fill the larger tank?

3m × 4m × 5m

6m × 12m × 10m

A 40 min   B 60 min   C 90 min
D 2 hours   E 4 hours

P59 My granny can carry 600 sprouts in a suitcase measuring 30 cm × 50 cm × 12 cm.
How many could she carry in a larger suitcase which measures 50 cm × 60 cm × 18 cm?

A 900   B 1200   C 1800   D 2700   E 3600

P60 The perimeter of the outer square is 32 cm, and the perimeter of the inner square is 24 cm. If the four rectangles are all identical, what is the perimeter of the shaded shape?

A 16 cm   B 20 cm   C 24 cm   D 28 cm   E 32 cm

P61 Lara is a ladybird who weighs 0.02 g. Clara is a cormorant who weighs 2.02 kg.
How many times heavier than Lara is Clara?

A 101   B 1010   C 10 101
D 101 000   E 101 010

Puzzling Problems

P62 Tyler Wall wants to tile her kitchen by repeating this 4 × 4 pattern of tiles, starting from the bottom left corner and working across and up. The area that she wants to tile measures 18 tiles across and 14 tiles up. Tiles are sold in packs of 10. How many **packs** of white tiles will she need to buy? *unsure*

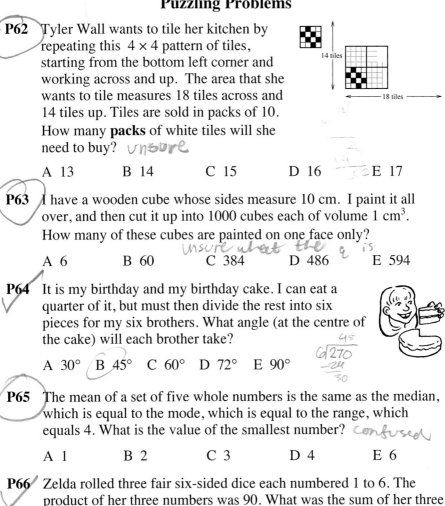

A 13   B 14   C 15   D 16   E 17

P63 I have a wooden cube whose sides measure 10 cm. I paint it all over, and then cut it up into 1000 cubes each of volume 1 cm^3. How many of these cubes are painted on one face only? *unsure what the q is*

A 6   B 60   C 384   D 486   E 594

P64 It is my birthday and my birthday cake. I can eat a quarter of it, but must then divide the rest into six pieces for my six brothers. What angle (at the centre of the cake) will each brother take?

A 30°   B 45°   C 60°   D 72°   E 90°

P65 The mean of a set of five whole numbers is the same as the median, which is equal to the mode, which is equal to the range, which equals 4. What is the value of the smallest number? *confused*

A 1   B 2   C 3   D 4   E 6

P66 Zelda rolled three fair six-sided dice each numbered 1 to 6. The product of her three numbers was 90. What was the sum of her three numbers?

A 12   B 14   C 15   D 16   E impossible to tell

Puzzling Problems

P67 A simple lock on a safe uses two numbers. Each can be from 1 to 6. To enter the safe, any even number and any odd number is needed (in any order). What is the probability that someone choosing numbers at random will open the safe in one go?

A $\dfrac{1}{36}$ B $\dfrac{1}{6}$ C $\dfrac{1}{4}$ D $\dfrac{1}{2}$ E $\dfrac{2}{3}$

P68 Dhiran has forgotten the last of the four digits of the code for his bicycle lock. He knows that the first three digits are 451 and that the code number is a multiple of 3, but not a multiple of 5 or of 9. What is the last digit?

A 1 B 2 C 3 D 5 E 8

P69 There are 18 chocolates in Swee Tuth's box, 2 each of 9 flavours. She likes only 6 of the flavours. If she picks a chocolate at random, what is the probability of her getting one she doesn't like?

A $\dfrac{2}{9}$ B $\dfrac{1}{3}$ C $\dfrac{4}{9}$ D $\dfrac{1}{2}$ E $\dfrac{2}{3}$

P70 The table shows the results of a survey in which 60 boys and 60 girls were asked what colour of dress girls should wear.

	blue	pink	black
girls	12	6	42
boys	15	24	21

What percent of boys thought girls should wear pink?

A 5% B 10% C 20% D 40% E 100%

Puzzling Problems

P71 Pupils in Mrs Madir's class were asked about their favourite colour of jelly baby. The results are shown in this bar graph. Which two colours taken together are the favourites of exactly 50% of the class?

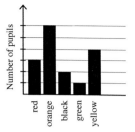

A black and orange
B green and orange   C orange and yellow
D red and orange   E red and yellow

P72 The graph that Polly drew showed the more sports that children played the more likely they were to be good at football. However, she found one child was an exception.
Which of the following scatter graphs represents her results best?

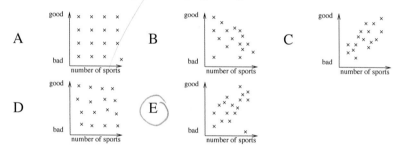

Very Challenging Problems

V1 Which of the following is the largest?

A $654 \div (32 + 1)$ B $654 \div (3 + 21)$ C $654 \div (32 \times 1)$
D $654 \div (32 - 1)$ E $654 \div 321$

V2 Karl Lecter has been collecting 1p, 2p and 5p coins in a jar. All but 10 of his coins are 1p coins, all but 10 are 2p coins, and all but 10 are 5p coins. How much money does he have?

A 8p   B 10p   C 25p   D 40p   E 80p

V3 What is the second to last digit when 5^7 is calculated?

A 0   B 2   C 5   D 6   E 8

V4 Kim writes all the counting numbers from 1 to 100 in order without leaving any gaps:

$$123456789101112131415\ldots$$

What is the 100th digit that Kim writes?

A 1   B 3   C 5   D 7   E 9

V5 Aunty Histamine needs to take 15 ml of medicine 3 times a day for 2 weeks.
How much medicine will she have taken when she has finished?

A 42 ml   B 210 ml   C 315 ml   D 500 ml   E 630 ml

V6 In a park I can see people and dogs out for walk. I see 13 noses and 36 legs.
How many tails are there in the park?

A 5   B 8   C 13   D 20   E 49

V7 In a computer game, the code to the door into *Cyberheaven* has four digits and is divisible by 13, 17 and 19. What is the number?

A 4191   B 4193   C 4195   D 4197   E 4199

Very Challenging Problems

V8 A city banker gets a bonus of £2 million. He says, "I will give my five children £1000 each, and my wife £5000". How much does he keep for himself?

A £100 B £1 990 C £19 900

D £199 000 E £1 990 000

V9 Doris has a collection of 10p and 1p coins in her money box. She has less than £1 altogether, an odd number of 10p coins and fewer than ten 1p coins. The total amount of her money is a square number of pence.
How many 1p coins does she have?

A 1 B 4 C 5 D 6 E impossible to say

V10 Yesterday Peggy Gregg bought 3 cakes and 3 doughnuts for £1.17.
Today she bought 6 cakes and 4 doughnuts for £2.06.
How much will 3 cakes and one doughnut cost her tomorrow?

A 39p B 89p C £1.08 D £1.17 E £2.06

V11 If I write all the whole numbers from 1 to 100 in words, how many times will I write the letter V?

A 19 B 29 C 30 D 31 E 32

V12 In the long multiplication shown on the right, what is the total of the four digits that should go in the four boxes?

A 26 B 27 C 28 D 29 E 30

$$
\begin{array}{r}
6\,\square \\
\times\ \square\,7 \\
\hline
\square\,8\,3 \\
\square\,5\,2\,0 \\
\hline
6\,0\,0\,3
\end{array}
$$

V13 Lycra Mike needs to cycle 24 miles to Ped L. Pusher's house in 2 hours. He does the first 12 miles at 6 mph. How fast must he now go to get to the house on time?

A 3 mph B 6 mph C 12 mph D 24 mph E impossible

Very Challenging Problems

V14 On Monday, Mr Brighton Urly got up at 7.15 am, started work at $(x + 2)$ am and finished work at $(x - 2)$ pm. How many hours did he work on Monday?

    A $24 - 2x$ B $12 - x$ C 4   D $2x - 4$ E 8

V15 The octagon shown shaded here is formed from two identical overlapping squares. Each square has sides of length 8 cm and the area of each triangle is 2 cm^2. What is the area of the octagon?

    A 8 cm^2 B 16 cm^2 C 32 cm^2 D 56 cm^2 E 62 cm^2

V16 Four teenage tadpoles weigh the same as three jolly jellyfish; two jolly jellyfish weigh the same as five nuclear newts. How many nuclear newts weigh the same as forty teenage tadpoles?

    A 30   B 40   C 50   D 60   E 75

V17 When a pot of plum jam is two-thirds full, it weighs 400 g. When it is only one-third full it weighs 250 g.
How much does a full pot of plum jam weigh?

    A 150 g   B 500 g   C 550 g   D 600 g   E 750 g

V18 Anita Room is going to do some tidying. She can tidy 2 big rooms in the same time as it takes to tidy 3 small rooms. She can tidy 1 big room and 3 small rooms in 90 minutes.
How long does it take her to tidy 3 big rooms and 6 small rooms?

    A 3 hours 30 minutes   B 4 hours
    C 4 hours 30 minutes   D 5 hours
    E 5 hours 30 minutes

Very Challenging Problems

V19 Jemima had some identical square cards. She had fewer than 200 altogether. She tried to arrange them in rows of 4 but had 1 left over. She tried rows of 5 and then rows of 6, but each time she had one card left. Finally she discovered that she could arrange them to form one large solid square . How many cards were on each side of the square?

    A 7   B 8   C 9   D 10   E 11

V20 A cleaner earns £16 000 a year, a teacher earns £28 000 a year and a banker earns £72 000. Suppose they all need £12 000 to pay the basic costs of living. If they all take away the basic costs of living from their salaries, which of the following ratios (cleaner : teacher : banker) best describes the money they are left with for other spending?

    A 1:1:1   B 1:2:3   C 1:4:15   D 4:7:18   E 16:28:72

V21 Milly, her little sister Tilly, their mother Jilly and their grandmother Lilly have ages that are different cube numbers. Lilly is not yet 100. How old was Lilly when Milly was born?

    A 19   B 40   C 48   D 56   E 64

V22 Dee Vide and her brother Horatio have the same birthday. One year, Dee noticed that she was 5 times her brother's age. Later, she was four times his age, and then 3 times. This year, she was exactly twice his age. As they are both less than 40 years old, how old is Horatio now?

    A 4   B 6   C 8   D 9   E 12

V23 Usain Bolt holds the Olympic record for the 200 m at 19.3 seconds.
If he can improve his time in the 2012 Olympics by 2%, what would be his new time?

    A 0.386 sec   B 15.44 sec   C 18.914 sec
    D 19.107 sec   E 19.686 sec

Very Challenging Problems

V24 A cheetah has been recorded travelling at 72 miles per hour.
A snail can travel for 30 hours and cover a mile.
How many times faster is the cheetah compared with the snail?

    A 24   B 216   C 240   D 2160   E 2400

V25 Two short model cars start at the same time on opposite sides of a race track. One car can complete a circuit of the track in 9 seconds, the other in 12 seconds. How long after starting will one car catch up with the other?

    A 12 secs   B 18 secs   C 20 secs   D 24 secs   E 48 secs

V26 Miss A. Stitch's knitting club meets on the first Mondays of June, July and August. Last summer, the dates were 7th June, 5th July and 2nd August. The total of these dates is $7 + 5 + 2 = 14$. What is the highest possible total for the dates of the first Monday of the months of June, July and August?

    A 14   B 15   C 16   D 17   E 18

V27 Our school has agreed to reduce its energy use over the next three years. Each year, the amount of energy used will be 10% less than the previous year. What will the total percentage reduction in energy use over the three years be?

    A 27.1   B 30   C 70   D 72.1   E 100

V28 Suppose $a + b = 1$ and $c + d = 2$ and $e + f = 3$ and $b + c + d + e + f = 5$.
What is the value of a ?

    A −2   B −1   C 0   D 1   E 2

V29 You are given that $p = 3$, $q = 2$ and that $p^3 \times q^2 \times r = 432$.
What is the value of r?

    A 2   B 3   C 4   D 6   E 8

Easy Problems – Answers and Notes

E1 **C** **24**

$1 \times 2 \times 3 \times 4 = 24$.

E2 **A** **16**

One quarter of 16 is 4.

E3 **C** **15**

$50 = 2 \times 5 \times 5$. 3 is not in the list of factors so 15 cannot be a factor.

The prime factors of 50 are shown by $2 \times 5 \times 5$. The factors of 50 can be made by combining these $(2, 5, 10, 25, 50)$. 1 is also a factor. Pupils could explore other numbers to find their prime factors and their complete set of factors.

E4 **A** **55**

Pupils could add up the ten numbers directly. Or add the first and the last to make 11, the second and the second to last to make another 11 and so on, getting five groups totalling 11 each. The sum of the ten numbers is therefore $5 \times 11 = 55$.

Here are some similar problems:

a) $10 + 11 + 12 + 13 + 14 + 15 + 16 + 17 + 18 + 19$

b) $23 + 24 + 25 + 26 + 27 + 28 + 29 + 30 + 31 + 32$

c) $10 + 12 + 14 + 16 + 18 + 20 + 22 + 24 + 26 + 28$

d) $35 + 38 + 41 + 44 + 47 + 50 + 53 + 56 + 59 + 62$.

E5 **D** **18**

One dozen is 12, so a dozen and a half is 18.

E6 **D** **20**

The parrot will learn five words four times each hour – 20 new words.

Pupils could make up some really silly problems such as: If I can eat one hard boiled egg in one minute, how many can I eat in one hour?

E7 **B** **5**

Seven years ago Alacoe was 6 years old so last year she was 5 years old.

Easy Problems – Answers and Notes

E8 A 3.4 m

(B) and (C) are equal, as are (D) and (E).

E9 C 7

Seven days in a week so seven apples.

E10 C 396

$6 \times 66 = 396$.

Can your pupils think of anything with an odd number of legs?
{Such as a three-legged stool}

E11 D $\frac{5}{9}$

Five small squares out of nine are shaded black.

E12 D 23

$5 \times 2 + 3 \times 3 + 4 = 23$.

E13 E 999

$111 + 333 + 555 = 999$.

E14 C 2

21 000 and 100 014 are larger than 11 000; the others are not.

E15 E no difference

Suppose one toy costs 50p with none of the offers. Working through the first four alternatives gives 25p for one toy. So the answer is E.

E16 B £530

53 000 pence equals £530.

E17 D 20

There are 20 red and 10 blue counters.

E18 C 30

Numbers with a factor of 2 and 5 are the multiples of 10; the smallest positive such number with a factor of 3 is 30. This is the lowest common multiple (LCM) of 2, 3 and 5.

If you continued with only prime numbers, the LCM would simply be the product of all of them. But how big is the LCM of 2, 3, 4, 5, 6, 7, 8, 9 and 10?

Easy Problems – Answers and Notes

E19 B   2

If there is one answer that the machine always gives, we might try starting off with 0: $0 \rightarrow 3 \rightarrow 6 \rightarrow 6 \rightarrow 2$. Other inputs produce the same result: $3.7 \rightarrow 6.7 \rightarrow 13.4 \rightarrow 6 \rightarrow 2$. Using algebra, we can see why the machine always gives the answer 2: if you were to start with a number n, then the sequence becomes: $n \rightarrow n + 3 \rightarrow 2n + 6 \rightarrow 2n + 6 - 2n = 6 \rightarrow 2$.

Can you design another complex machine that gives the same answer whatever number is put in?

E20 B   11

The prime numbers less than 20 are 2, 3, 5, 7, 11, 13, 17 and 19. You might like children to investigate what happens when different primes have their digits reversed! Are there other prime numbers that remain the same number when their digits are reversed? (101 is one) Why are there none larger than 11 but less than 100?

E21 C   £59.90

There are several ways of sorting this out. Ten pizzas @ £6 less 10p is probably the easiest. Or multiply £5.99 by 10 by 'moving the point'.

E22 C   £1

The increase is 10p a journey, twice a day. So the total increase is £1.

E23 D   9.1

The arrow points midway between 9.0 and 9.2 and so to 9.1.

E24 E   8

Counting the notes of music gives $2 + \frac{1}{2} + \frac{1}{2} + 4 + 1 = 8$ beats. Pupils can look at a few short pieces of music, noticing the equal number of beats in each bar for that piece of music. They could even write some music!

E25 B   40 min

From 5.15 pm to 6.05 pm is 50 minutes, of which 10 minutes is a break.

Easy Problems – Answers and Notes

E26 A   −16°C

(−8) − 8 = −16. The number line helps here.

E27 E   4 > 3

Only 4 > 3 is correct.

E28 A   circle

All the other shapes are also in the picture of a bird.
Pupils can design other animals and objects with mathematical shapes.

E29 E   32

The complete patio will be 8 × 4 and will have 32 slabs.

E30 D   Triangle

The shape with the smallest number of sides will have sides of the largest triangle. So the triangle will have sides of the longest length (20 cm).

E31 C

C does not have eight sides. It is a heptagon.

E32 E   CUBE

There is no complete word which has a single symmetry, but all the individual letters in **CUBE** have mirror symmetry.

E33 E   2 triangles

Many different shapes can be found but not two triangles.

E34 E

Try it with a paper rectangle!

E35 B   4

$x = 11 − 7 = 4$ cm.

E36 D   22

A 3 × 3 × 3 cube requires 27 smaller cubes, so Finn needs 27 − 5 = 22 more.

Easy Problems – Answers and Notes

E37 D Polecat, head down looking to the right

The polecat has been rotated 90° clockwise and then reflected in a vertical axis.

E38 B 2

The first and third patterns have no line of symmetry (look carefully at the third). The second and fifth have one. The fourth has six. The symbols: humanism, Christianity, Islam, Judaism and Sikhism.

E39 E 24

The maximum score with one die is 6, so for four dice it will be 24.

Pupils can investigate the 'most popular' total when two dice are rolled.

E40 E 6

If we label from left to right the three obvious rectangles **P**, **Q** and **R**, we can see that **P** and **Q** together form another, as do **Q** and **R**, and also **P** and **Q** and **R**.

One could consider the diagram on the left and spot a connection with triangular numbers. If you consider the number of rectangles (including squares, of course) in the diagram on the right you get a nice combination of square and triangular numbers.

E41 B 14

Pupils have to be methodical to get this one correct!

E42 A impossible

3 or 4 eggs in a minute, but surely not 1000! That must be impossible.

Instead of a thousand eggs, what is the probability that a pupil could eat these numbers of eggs in a minute? 1, 2, 5, 8, 20.

Easy Problems – Answers and Notes

E43 D 6

Pupils can draw and list all the possibilities. Or consider that you can use three colours in the first section, leaving two for the next and one for colour for the final. This gives 6 possibilities.

How many different badges could be made if a badge used four colours, or more? There is a pattern here. If the number of colours used in making a badge is n, then the numbers of badges that can be made is $n \times (n - 1) \times (n - 2) \times \ldots \times 1$.

E44 B very unlikely

We have no evidence that a music teacher has been hit by bird poo, but it is not impossible.

Can pupils make up examples of problems which have the different probability outcomes used in this question?

Harder Problems – Answers and Notes

H1   **A**   **0.00001**

This is the longest number but the smallest in value.

H2   **C**   **300**

At each junction half the children choose each alternative. Children could extend this diagram, or make some of the roads cross. How many children would then arrive at each (new) point?

H3   **C**   **The only correct answer is C**

A: $2 \times 0 \times 14 = 0$ B: $2 + 0 \times 14 = 2 + 0 = 2$

C: $(2 + 0) \times 14 = 2 \times 14 = 28$ D: $2 + 0 + 14 = 16$

E: $2 \times 0 + 14 = 0 + 14 = 14$

H4   **C**   **10 days**

In one day, Willy needs 4×7.5 ml $= 30$ ml. So the bottle will last $300 \div 30 = 10$ days.

H5   **C**   **15**

30 seconds is one-tenth of 5 minutes so one-tenth of the heads will be stitched on.

H6   **B**   **90 cm**

After the first bounce the ball will rise to 120 cm, and then to 90 cm.

H7   **D**   **275 000**

A quarter of a million is 250 000, and 10% of this is 25 000; $250\,000 + 25\,000 = 275\,000$.

H8   **B**   **£1.60**

Two $7\frac{1}{2}$ minutes make up 15 minutes, so in one hour I have to pay 8 times 20p $= £1.60$.

H9   **B**   **75p**

Five coffees cost $5 \times 90p = £4.50$. Then she gets one free coffee. So she effectively pays $£4.50 \div 6 = 75p$ per cup.

Investigate other 'special offers' and 'bargains' in the local shops.

Harder Problems – Answers and Notes

H10 D 204

$11 \times 17 = 187$, but $12 \times 17 = 204$ is closer to 200.

H11 C 5

Every number whose units digit is 5 is a multiple of 5, so no number greater than 10 can be prime. On the other hand, 11, 23, 37 and 59 are examples of prime numbers ending in 1, 3, 7 and 9. When we think about the units digits of prime numbers, we are also considering what remainder there could be when dividing by ten. You might also consider what remainder there might be if instead you divide a prime number by 6: for primes greater than 3 the remainder cannot be an even number (as then the prime would also be even); nor can it be 3 (as then the prime would be a multiple of 3). Hence the only remainders you can get when dividing a prime number by 6 are 1 or 5 (mathematicians say that prime numbers greater than 3 are either $6n + 1$ or $6n + 5$).

H12 B 21

Of the factor pairs for 90 ($1 \times 90, 2 \times 45, 3 \times 30, 5 \times 18, 6 \times 15$ and 9×10) only 6 and 15 have a difference of 9; their sum is 21.

H13 C 8

$2012 = 2 \times 2 \times 503$. So its factors are 2, 4, 503 and 1006, but not 8.

Will there be a question like this in the next PMC? What are the factors of 2013? Is 33 a factor? Is 671 a factor? When is the next prime year? (2017)

H14 C 3

The horses need 27 gallons a day. That means Sue needs 7 containers. But she only has 3, so she has to make 3 trips in the car – the last trip with only one container (or two trips with 2 containers).

H15 D 39

Marcus goes to school on Tuesdays, Wednesdays and Thursdays, so there are $3 \times 13 = 39$ days in the term.

Harder Problems – Answers and Notes

H16 C 10

Pupils can work through the responses until they get one that works! Or use inverses: 8 → 16 → 20 → 10.

Pupils might be able to design problems like this which always end up with the same number. Here is one: think of a number; multiply by 4; add 8; halve the answer; and take away twice the original number. The answer is always four.

H17 D 154

Two numbers adding to 25 with a difference of 3 must be 11 and 14. The product of their ages is 11 × 14 = 154.

H18 B 100 000

6650 km ÷ 61 m is approximately 6 300 000 ÷ 63 = 100 000.

H19 E 64

The square numbers are 4, 9 and 64. The cube numbers are 8, 27 and 64. The only one which is both is 64.

H20 B 3

The total of the ages now is 88, that is 12 years under 100. The total increases by 4 each year, so their ages will add up to 100 in 12 ÷ 4 = 3 years.

H21 D 180 000

In a year of 365 days, the number of bags is 365 × 500 (≈ 180 000).

What if you were to consider the whole of the UK and assume that half the population will take one new plastic bag each week – how many bags would this amount to each year? In fact, in 2012, some 6.5 billion bags were given away by major supermarkets (about 250 for each UK household), though this number is decreasing [source: www.wrap.org.uk].

H22 E £6 ÷ 7

£6 divided by 7 gives 85p each with 5p left over.

What if Robyn shares £7 with 8 people, or £8 with 9 people, and so on. Will there be any patterns resulting in the amounts of money Robyn is allowed to keep?

Harder Problems – Answers and Notes

H23 C 45p

Dolores starts with £1, spends £1.50. So she then has −30p. She finds 75p and now has 45p.

It would seem that our world does not allow children to have a negative amount of money (unless you include loans). But mathematicians have often used seemingly impossible ideas and then they turn out to be most useful. An example is the use of the symbol $\sqrt{2}$ to represent an infinite decimal which is impossible to write down without something like $\sqrt{}$. Or the number i to represent $\sqrt{-1}$.

Here is another 'silly' sum: I have only one hour before bedtime. How much spare time will I have if I do homework (35min), text my girlfriend (10min), and then send some emails when having a bath (27min)?

H24 C 14 313

The sum is $13\,000 + 1300 + 13 = 14\,313$.

H25 C April

If 13th January is a Friday, the 13th February will be a Monday (January has 31 days which is four weeks and three days). February 2012 is a leap year (29 days), so 13th March will be a Tuesday. March has 31 days, so 13th April will move 3 days further and will be a Friday. This is the 'next' Friday the thirteenth.

H26 B 245

The journey takes 90 minutes to midday and 170 after midday which is a total of 260 minutes. It stops for 15 minutes and so it is moving for 245 minutes.

H27 C £1

The cost of 45 single copies is £4.50, whereas 50 copies will be £3.50.

H28 B 30

The small hand is on 11 and the large hand is on 12. So the angle between the two hands is $360° ÷ 12 = 30°$.

What would the angle be at half past eleven? Half past twelve?

46

Harder Problems – Answers and Notes

H29 C 25 minutes

Stopping at four stations takes $4 \times 45\,\text{sec} = 180\,\text{sec} = 3\,\text{min}$.
There are 28 minutes between 10.37 and 11.05 so the train is
moving for $28 - 3 = 25$ minutes.

H30 D 10 mph

Speedy cycles half a mile in 3 minutes, and so 1 mile in 6
minutes.

H31 E 120

Four circuits of the track make 1 km so 120 circuits make 30 km.

H32 C Wednesday

There are 30 days in November; that is 4 weeks and two days. So
the 1st December is on a Wednesday.

Pupils may be able to amaze their friends by calculating the day
of a week years ahead. There are normally 365 days in each year.
$365 \div 7$ gives 52 weeks and one day. So, unless it is a leap year,
a birthday one year will be on the next day of the week in the
following year. In ten years ahead, a birthday will be ten days
ahead plus the number of leap years in these ten years.

H33 C Henry III

Henry 1 (36 yrs), Henry II (35 yrs), Henry III (56 yrs), Henry IV
(14 yrs) and Henry V (9 yrs).

Other kings and queens of Britain may have been on the throne
for longer than Henry III. Has our present queen been on the
throne the longest so far?

H34 C 5

Taking 2 #s away from either side tells us that $15 = 3 \times \#$.
So $\# = 5$. Other children may prefer to use trial and error!

H35 C 4

We need to find a number with the same number of letters in its
name as its value. The only number to satisfy this condition is 4.

Harder Problems – Answers and Notes

H36 B $p - q + r$

The algebraic lengths might worry some pupils, but replacing them with numbers might make it clear that the distance x is $p - q + r$.

Pupils can write algebraic expressions for the lengths marked by d, e and f in terms of the other letters.

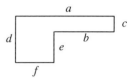

Can they write an algebraic expression for the area of the shape? In a few different ways?

H37 B 20 m

Counting along the midpoints of the paving stones gives 20 m. How fast would a snail actually crawl? How long would it take the snail to travel this route?

H38 D hexagonal prism

The number of edges for these shapes is A (6), cube (12), square-based pyramid (8), hexagonal prism (18) and octahedron (12). Which of the shapes in the question have the largest number of faces, or vertices? Do you think a curved side can be called a face (e.g. on a cylinder, sphere)?

H39 C 3

There are three sets of parallel lines with four lines in each set.

H40 A Monday

June has 30 days ($4 \times 7 + 2$) so that the day of the week moves on two days between June and July.

H41 A 5

Five more matches are needed to make the edges from the base to the point at the top.

Your pupils can explore how many matches are needed for a base of 3 or 4 matches? Be careful if you have a base of six or more! Why?

Harder Problems – Answers and Notes

H42 D Teflon

Neoprene lies with the month of the year; Nylon lies with the day of the month; Formica lies because of the year (2012) and Trogamid lies because there are only 28 or 29 days in each February.

Can your pupils think of other reasons why someone might get a birth date wrong? For example, give a year such as 1856 or 3011.

H43 A $\dfrac{1}{8}$

Mr Oak uses 'solid' $1 - \left(\frac{1}{2} + \frac{1}{4} + \frac{1}{8}\right) = \frac{1}{8}$ of the time. Pupils could add the fractions in the bracket using equivalent fractions, then subtract from 1.

The fractions in this problem provide an easy insight into the situation in which the sum of an infinite number of numbers is finite. In this case, adding more of these fractions will only get closer to the number 2. Pupils might consider if the sum can actually reach 2; if the sum did continue for ever, would it reach 2?

There are other sums which, if continued for ever, would reach a finite number:

$$\frac{1}{3} + \frac{1}{9} + \frac{1}{27} + \frac{1}{81} + \ldots .$$

Pupils might instigate what happens in this case:

$$1 + \frac{1}{2} + \frac{1}{3} + \frac{1}{4} + \frac{1}{5} + \ldots .$$

H44 D 2000

It will take Sennet $8 \times 100 + 12 \times 100 = 800 + 1200 = 2000$ seconds. More easily – it will take 20 seconds for each foot and $20 \times 100 = 2000$ seconds.

H45 E 69

Granny's age is $2 \times 4 \times 8 + 5 = 69$.

Pupils could work out other ways of calculating the ages of their grannies and granddads.

Harder Problems – Answers and Notes

H46 B 4

He saves £1 + £2 + £4 + £8 = £15. So it takes Owen four weeks.
Pupils can examine the targets when extending this problem for
more weeks. The numbers obtained (1, 3, 7, 15, 31, 63 ...) are all
one less than powers of 2. Pupils may be able to calculate
answers to the longer problems without doing the addition sums.

H47 A 1000

One revolution of the wheel takes the car 1 metre forward. So it
will need 1000 revolutions to make 1 km.

H48 B 17

The final cuboid will contain $4 \times 3 \times 5 = 60$ cubes. He used
43 and will need 17 more.

H49 D ○

You pass through these numbers: 6, 1, 2, 3, 3, 1, 1 to the
octagon.
Can you pass through every hexagon when going in and coming
out at the square sign?

H50 B 9 cm

The longest side is 12 cm, leaving a total of 18 cm for the other
two equal sides. That is 9 cm each.
Try to find these lengths in each of these problems about
isosceles triangles.
a) the perimeter is 30 cm; the longest side is 14 cm; find the
   lengths of the shortest sides.
b) the perimeter is 30 cm; the longest side is 10 cm; find the
   lengths of the shortest sides. What happens here?
c) the perimeter is 30 cm; one of the shortest sides is 5 cm; find
   the longest side. What happens here?
d) the perimeter is 30 cm; one of the shortest sides is 18 cm;
   find the longest side. What happens here?

Harder Problems – Answers and Notes

H51 D $\frac{2}{3}$

All six triangles are equal in area (not very obvious but thinking about the four in the rectangle helps). Four out of six are shaded.

H52 C 40 cm²

Adding the diagonals to the smaller square shows that the area of the larger square is twice the area of the smaller square.

H53 C $\frac{1}{2}$

Each of the unshaded triangles occupies a quarter of the square (as shown on the right); so the fraction of the room in which the camera can detect is $1 - \left(2 \times \frac{1}{4}\right) = \frac{1}{2}$.

How would it be possible in a similar way for the camera to detect objects in $\frac{2}{3}$ of the room?

H54 B 9

In three of the four outcomes, a chocolate is taken from the box. For a 'fair' spinner, we would expect a chocolate to remain in the box after about one of every four spins. So for 36 spins, we would expect about a quarter of 36 (= 9) chocolates to be left in the box.

H55 B

The shaded areas are half in shapes A, C and D. The shaded area in B is clearly more than half (compare with C). The shaded area in E is less than that of B so the largest shaded area is in shape B. Pupils can draw several different patterns which will shade in half of each square. Or even try other fractions too.

H56 A rhombus

A rhombus would need two equal sides in both original triangles, so a rhombus is impossible with these triangles.

Pupils could start with identical but different shapes, such as two squares, two equilateral triangles, two isosceles triangles or two parallelograms, and see what shapes they can get.

H57 E   12

Cutting off a small triangle adds one extra side to each of the six sides of the hexagon. So after cutting off the six small triangles there will be 12 sides.

The polygon now has 12 edges. If the process was repeated, there would be 24 edges.

And if this carried indefinitely, how many edges would there be and approximately what would the shape of the polygon now look like?

H58 C   15 cm^3

The original cube has a volume of $3 \times 3 \times 3 = 27$ cm^3, from which are removed four cuboids each of volume 3 cm^3. So the remaining solid has volume of $27 - 3 \times 4 = 15$ cm^3.

Alternatively, the cross-sectional cross has an area of 5 cm^2 and length 3 cm, hence the volume is $5 \times 3 = 15$ cm^3.

H59 A

After I get out the depth of water will fall almost instantly, and then gradually as the water drains away.

If the axes were not labelled as time and depth, but had different labels, what real events could the other graphs in this question represent?

H60 B   5

The only multiple of 7 between 240 and 249 is 245.

You will know how to test whether a number is a multiple of 5 or 10, or 3 or 9, or 4 or 8, without doing the actual calculation for dividing. There are divisibility rules for many numbers, including for divisibility by 7. See
www.mathsisfun.com/divisibility-rules.html
or (to take it even further)
www.jamestanton.com/?p=577.

Harder Problems – Answers and Notes

H61 C South

After every 4 "Right turns" the troops will be facing North again; so after 68 turns they are facing North, after 69 turns East, and after 70 turns South.

Puzzling Problems – Answers and Notes

P1 B 900

This question is about digits not numbers. Try adding the units digits separately and see what happens. Then see how many tens digits there are, and what they add up to.

P2 D 68

After the first three numbers, each number is the sum of the previous three numbers. So the next number is
$11 + 20 + 37 = 68$.

P3 B 20

This looks very difficult but pupils might notice that the second bracket (on the top) equals 992 and can cancel down with the 992 on the bottom leaving $3 + 7 + 10 = 20$. This is a problem quoted in *Lewis Carroll in Numberland* by Robin Wilson, Penguin (2009).

P4 B 36 years

Even square numbers are 4, 16, 36, 64 and 100. A gap of 48 years between Bhupinder and her grandmother means that Bhupinder is now 16 and granny 64. Her mother is therefore 36 years old.

What if Bhupinder and her relatives had ages that were all prime numbers?

P5 A 5

The sum of 4 children's ages is 42, so pupils could think that they will be about 10 years old each, as a start to solving the problem. So, with two years apart for the boys and the girls, a first estimate could be 14, 12, 8, 6 which totals 40. An adjustment to this would give us 16, 14, 7, 5 which totals 42 and meets the criteria that the younger boy's age is twice the older girl's age.

P6 C Isobel

Taking the sentences in order and using < as 'shorter than', we have: S < I, then S < E < I and finally S < E < I < A < R.

Puzzling Problems – Answers and Notes

P7   D   4

4 wins (12 points) + 1 draw (2 points) + 2 losses (2 points) total 16 points altogether.

Try inventing different scoring systems for the chess challenge. Are there any scoring systems that work particularly well for good players or for bad players?

P8   D   2017

2012 is divisible by 2. 2013 is divisible by 3. 2015 is divisible by 5. 2019 is divisible by 3. But 2017 is a prime number.

P9   B   20p

Pupils can write out these sentences in full English but we can use simple algebra: $2c + d = 80p$ and $3c + 2d = 130p$. If we double the first equation we get $4c + 2d = 160p$. Subtracting we can see that $c = 30p$. That means that $d = 20p$.

How about these:

a) $2c + 2d = 80p$ and $3d + 2d = 120p$ ($c = 40p$ and $d = 0p$)
b) $2c + 2d = 80p$ and $2c + 3d = 120p$ (cakes are free!)
c) $2c + 2d = 80p$ and $3d + 3d = 120p$ (impossible to calculate)

Pupils could make up their own similar problems and see what happens.

P10   D   1201

2011 divided by 4 gives a remainder of 3, so the last three digits are 201 and so the first digit must be 1. Hence 1201.

Experiment with different sequences of numbers and shapes. Can children guess what numbers or shapes will come in what position?

P11   C   8

There are six chapters containing a total of 48 pages. So there are $48 \div 6 = 8$ pages in each chapter.

P12   D   12

The minute hand takes one hour per revolution; the hour hand takes twelve hours. So the minute hand goes round 12 times faster than the hour hand.

Puzzling Problems – Answers and Notes

P13 E 24

If the car can travel 48 miles with 1 gallon of petrol, half a gallon will take it 24 miles.

P14 B 183 kg

Adding all three totals gives 366 kg, which is the weight of two Dads, two Mums and two Alices. So one of each must weigh 366 ÷ 2 = 183 kg.

Can children work out how much each person weighs?

P15 C 99

There are palindromic numbers before the year 3000, so let us start with a 2. The number must end with a 2, and the two middle numbers must be as low as possible and the same. The year 2002 has passed, but 2112 has not. 2112 − 2013 = 99 years.

P16 A 9

The first year when this happens again is 2020, so in 9 years.

P17 E 16

$\sqrt{16}$ = 4, so the equation now looks like 4 + $\sqrt{n}$ = 8. This tells us that $\sqrt{n}$ must equal 4 so n = 16.

Here are some more nasty looking equations involving square roots!

a) $n = \sqrt{4} + \sqrt{4}$ (n = 4)   b) $5 = \sqrt{n} + 4$ (n = 1)
c) $8 = 13 - \sqrt{n}$ (n = 25)   d) $9 - \sqrt{n} = 5$ (n = 16)
e) $\sqrt{n} = n - 12$ (n = 16)

P18 D A multiple of 30

All prime numbers other than 2 are odd numbers. Multiples of 3 can be odd (3, 9, 15 etc.).

Some odd square numbers are 9, 25 and 49. The factors of three are 1 and 3, both odd. But all multiples of 30 are even.

Puzzling Problems – Answers and Notes

P19 D 6

Because 2, 19 and 53 are prime factors of 2014, the only other factors are these factors themselves or products of some of them. So there are 6 factors apart from 1 and 2014: 2, 19, $2 \times 19 = 38$, 53, $2 \times 53 = 106$ and $19 \times 53 = 1007$.

Not only is $2014 = 2 \times 19 \times 53$, but the year $2013 = 3 \times 11 \times 61$ and the year $2015 = 5 \times 13 \times 31$; they each have 8 factors.

When is the next year number to have exactly 8 factors? You'll be glad to know that you have not got to wait until $4102 = 2 \times 7 \times 293$.

P20 A 94

The largest single-digit prime number is 7 and the smallest three-digit prime number is 101; their difference is $101 - 7 = 94$.

On the other hand: what is the difference between the largest single-digit non-prime number and the smallest three-digit non-prime number?

P21 E 2017

2013 is divisible by 3. 2014 and 2016 are divisible by 2 and 2015 is divisible by 5. So 2017 must be the prime number but that can be checked.

P22 B 13

The two-digit primes less than 20 are 11, 13, 17 and 19. Reversing the digits gives 11, 31, 71 and 91. The only pair to give 403 when multiplied is 13 and 31.

P23 D 8

The digits of the number must add up to a multiple of 9 if the number is divisible by 9. $6 + 4 + 1 = 11$. The next multiple of 9 above 11 is 18, but © + ©, being equal, would be $3\frac{1}{2}$ each – no good. If the sum of the digits is 27, the © + © = 16 and © = 8.

P24 D 20

In a 24 day period, one foot needs 12 socks and the other needs 8 socks. The total is 20 socks.

Puzzling Problems – Answers and Notes

P25 D £30

Gus and Harry each paid £5 (total £10) to cover Ian's lunch. So each lunch cost £10. The total bill was therefore £30.

P26 E £360

£10 for 20 injections gives 50p for each. At his improved speed he can give $20 \times 36 = 720$ injections in 20 minutes. At 50p each he will earn £360.

P27 B one quarter

One way to tackle this question is to start with a number of strawberries for which we can easily find one third, one quarter and one sixth: 12 is the smallest. Then 4 are eaten by wasps, 3 by ants and 2 by a maggot, leaving 3 out of 12, or one quarter. Alternatively, one can think in fractions, though this amounts to the same thing:

$$1 - \frac{1}{3} - \frac{1}{4} - \frac{1}{6} = \frac{12}{12} - \frac{4}{12} - \frac{3}{12} - \frac{2}{12} = \frac{3}{12} = \frac{1}{4}.$$

P28 E 160 ml

When one has quarters of quarters, it helps to think in sixteenths. So four sixteenths of the bottle is stewed slime, and one quarter of the rest equals three sixteenths. Therefore, $\frac{9}{16}$ of the bottle is 90 ml and so the whole bottle is 160 ml.

Children might like to create their own versions of this problem, varying the fractions/proportions used of different ingredients.

Puzzling Problems – Answers and Notes

P29 D 36

The highest possible pile of tins is 80 cm, the height of 8 tins. As this pile is also 8 tins wide, the pile will also fit widthways in the window. The number of tins in each pile is a triangular number (not surprisingly), and the eighth triangular number is 36.

If the window is deep enough for it, Willy could stack the tins in the shape of a square based pyramid with, for instance, 9 on the bottom, 4 above that and 1 on the top. The numbers of tins he could use in each pyramid stack are known as square pyramidal numbers. For further details, see http://mathworld.wolfram.com/ SquarePyramidalNumber.html. If Willy preferred pyramids with triangular bases, the number of tins would be the tetrahedral numbers. Do you know of the connections between square numbers, triangular numbers, tetrahedral numbers and Pascal's triangle? If not, see www.mathsisfun.com/pascals-triangle.html

P30 E 20

Ten chairs will have units digit equal to 7, and ten chairs will have tens digits equal to 7. 10 + 10 = 20.

P31 C 7 weeks, 3 days

Marcus has been absent 20% of 190 days = 38 days. With a school week of 5 days, this is 7 weeks and 3 days.

P32 A 12

With three teachers missing, 20 are at the staff meeting. Five are asleep, and 20% of the remaining 15, three (20%) are texting. This leaves 23 − 3 − 5 − 3 = 12 teachers listening to the Head.

P33 D four fifths of a century

John was 13 at the time of the 1948 Olympics, so he was 13 + 52 minus 3 years old at the millennium, and so is 13 + 52 + 12 = 77 years old in 2012. That is $\frac{4}{5}$ of a century minus 3 years.

Puzzling Problems – Answers and Notes

P34 B 6

Since Tom runs one and a half times as fast as Jerry, Tom moves round the clock 3 places for every 2 for Jerry. We can consider their progress in the table below:

position on clock face

Tom	12	3	6	9	12	3	6
Jerry	6	8	10	12	2	4	6

Therefore the first time they meet is at the number 6.

P35 D 12.18 am

The time passed between 6 pm and 1 am is 7 hours, and in this time the second clock will have lost $7 \times 6 = 42$ minutes. So the time it will show is 12.18 am.

P36 C Wednesday

Luigi's birthday will be $34 + 43$ days after Julian's birthday. That is 77 days which is exactly eleven weeks. So Luigi's birthday will also be on a Wednesday.

If today is a Wednesday, what will be the day of the week in 1000 days? In one million days (that is about 2747 years' time) assuming the earth is still in one piece?

P37 A 30%

If there were 100 voters, half voted. Of this half, 60% of the 50 voters voted for the wining party. That is 60% of 50 = 30 voters. So 30 out of 100 voters voted for the winning party; i.e. 30%.

P38 C 3 4 5 6

Possible codes in which each number is one more than the previous digit are: 1 2 3 4, 2 3 4 5, 3 4 5 6, 4 5 6 7, 5 6 7 8 and 6 7 8 9. The only code here which is a multiple of four is 3 4 5 6.

P39 A Aled

Aled is stretched by 5 cm. Bertie, Daisy and Ethan are stretched by only 3 cm, so rule them out. That leaves just Aled and Carmen. Carmen is taller than Aled and so her stretch is proportionally smaller.

Puzzling Problems – Answers and Notes

P40 C   84 cm

Six equal gaps make up a decrease of $120 - 12 = 108$ cm. One gap is therefore 18 cm. So the third fountain from the left rises $120 - (18 \times 2) = 84$ cm.

P41 C   6

The Quads played 3 games, had no draws and lost one so they must have won 2 games. They therefore scored $2 \times 3 = 6$ points.

In the score sheet, several spaces have been left blank. On a similar score sheet, pupils can try to fill in as small a number of spaces as possible allowing others to calculate all the missing numbers. What is the smallest possible number of spaces that have to be filled in which will enable the rest to be completed?

P42 C   2

As $a + b + c = 10$ and $a + b = 6$, so $c = 4$. As $c + d = 6$, then $d = 2$. Without any further information, we cannot say for sure what the values of a and b are (as if there are 4 letters to find the value of, we must start with 4 equations in order to be able to work out all 4 values).

If we are limited to positive integers, how many possibilities are there for a and b? Pupils could investigate different equations which have a different number of unknown letters.

P43 B   16 cm²

The length of SQ is 2 cm and the length of QS is 6 cm. So triangle PRS has area 12 cm² and triangle QRS has area 4 cm². Therefore the area of triangle PQR is 16 cm².

P44 C   35°

Because triangle RQS is isosceles, angle RSQ = angle SRQ = 70°. Therefore we know that angle $QSP = 180° - 70° = 110°$. Triangle QSP is also isosceles, and so angle $SQP = x°$. Now, considering the three angles of triangle QSP, we have $x + x + 110 = 180$, and so $x° = 35°$.

Puzzling Problems – Answers and Notes

P45 D 110°

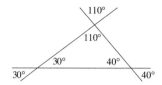

Children could draw and measure the angles in other similarly drawn triangles. Can they generalise their results?

P46 C right-angled scalene

The three angles of a triangle add up to 180°. In order for the ratio of the angles to be $1 : 2 : 3$, the largest has to be $\frac{3}{6} = \frac{1}{2}$ of the total, and therefore 90°. Since the smallest two angles are not equal, the triangle must be right-angled and scalene (its angles being 30°, 60° and 90°).

What type of *quadrilateral* has angles in the ratio of $1 : 1 : 1 : 1$, or $1 : 2 : 1 : 2$, or $1 : 2 : 2 : 1$, or $1 : 4 : 3 : 4$, or $1 : 7 : 1 : 3$? What about the *pentagon* whose angles are in the ratio $3 : 5 : 2 : 5 : 3$?

P47 B 18 m

Working from the point on the ground on the left, every 4 m along gives 2 m in height. The distance along the ground is 36 m, so the height of the tower is $9 \times 2 = 18$ m. Alternatively, by ratio, $\dfrac{h}{36} = \dfrac{2}{4}$ giving $h = 18$.

Here are two easy similar triangles. How long is the side marked *x*?

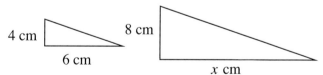

P48 C 90 cm³

Volume of wedge is 'area of cross-section' multiplied by width. Area of cross-section is $\frac{1}{2} \times 6 \text{ cm} \times 10 \text{ cm} = 30 \text{ cm}^2$. Volume is therefore $30 \text{ cm}^2 \times 3 \text{ cm} = 90 \text{ cm}^3$.

Puzzling Problems – Answers and Notes

P49 A 45%

The height of an equilateral triangle must be rather less than its side length. There are two triangles to each square, but the combined area of two triangles (forming a rhombus) must be less than that of a square. As a result, less than half of the tessellation is covered by triangles, and only option (A) is less than 50%.

The percentage covered by triangles is actually about 46.4%. Is it possible to change the triangles to isosceles triangles so that the tessellation is equally covered by triangles and squares?

P50 B $\dfrac{1}{4}$

Each smaller rectangle is half the area of the next larger one. So the area of the middle sized rectangle would be half of the complete one if it were not covered by the smallest rectangle. But the smallest rectangle has an area half of the complete white rectangle. So the area of the unshaded rectangle *ABCD* is $\frac{1}{4}$ of the whole rectangle.

P51 E 135°

Three angles meet at the point with the angle $x°$. One is 90° and the other two are interior angles of the octagons and are equal. Now $360° - 90° = 270°$ so $x° = 135°$.

P52 E 36 cm²

Thinking of an octagon fitted into a square (as shown on the right), one can see that each of the triangles has an area of $(10 \times 10 - 64) \div 4 = 9$. But each square comprises four triangles, so the area of each square is 4×9 cm² $= 36$ cm².

The diagram shows regular octagons and squares tessellating – what other combinations of several different regular polygons tessellate with each other? Can you find anything else out about semi-regular tessellations – what is the difference between regular and semi-regular tessellations? See the interactive site http://nrich.maths.org/4832

Puzzling Problems – Answers and Notes

P53 B   3 m²

Amy's rose bed will be 9 metres long and $\frac{1}{3}$ metre wide. Its area will be 9 m $\times \frac{1}{3}$ m = 3 m².

P54 A   4.5 m²

If the diagram is increased to make two squares, the difference in areas is 9 m². We need half that difference giving 4.5 m².

P55 C   24 cm

The longest side of each triangle is 5 cm and each of the shorter straight parts of the perimeter are 4 − 3 = 1 cm long. Therefore the perimeter of the whole shape is 4 × (5 + 1) = 24 cm.

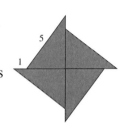

P56 C   3 and 12

If one imagines the shape (L) as a cuboid with a smaller cuboid (M) cut from it as shown on the right, the volume of the larger cuboid is 4 × 5 × 15 = 300 cm³. However, what is left (L) has a volume of 120 cm³, so

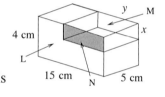

that shape M has a volume of 300 cm³ − 120 cm³ = 180 cm³. This means its cross-section (shaded N) has an area of 180 cm³ ÷ 5 cm = 36 cm². All of the pairs of dimensions will give an area of 36 cm², but only the pair x = 3 and y = 12 are smaller than the upright 4 cm and length 15 cm.

P57 D   400 ml

Alice has 10 litres = 10 000 ml, which when divided by 25 is 400 ml.

The author of Alice in Wonderland (where Alice meets the Hatter at the Mad Tea-Party) is Lewis Carroll, the pen-name of the mathematician Charles Lutwidge Dodgson (1832-1898) who taught at Oxford for 26 years and worked in the areas of geometry and logic.

Puzzling Problems – Answers and Notes

P58 E   4 hours

The small tank holds $3 \times 4 \times 5 = 60$ m³ of water. If the pipe can fill the tank in 20 minutes, it is giving $60 \div 20 = 3$ m³ water a minute. The large tank holds $6 \times 12 \times 10 = 720$ m³ of water. This will take $720 \div 3 = 240$ min $= 4$ hours to fill. Alternatively, using the ratio of lengths, breath and height, the time needed to fill the large tank will be
$20 \times 2 \times 3 \times 2 = 240$ min $= 4$ hours.

There are many different approaches to this question. Ask the pupils to compare and discuss their methods. Pupils could practise similar problems using the second method outlined in the above notes for the question.

P59 C   1800

Pupils might calculate the volumes of the two suitcases (18 000 cm³ and 54 000 cm³) and see that the volume of the larger is three times the volume of the smaller suitcase. So the number of sprouts will be $3 \times 600 = 1800$. But pupils might see that, in effect, one side has been doubled (to make 1200 sprouts) and then multiplied by $1\frac{1}{2}$ to make 1800 sprouts.

P60 A   16 cm

The sides of the two squares must be 8 cm and 6 cm. So the shaded rectangle is 7 cm by 1 cm giving a perimeter of 16 cm.

P61 B   101 000

Changing both masses into grams, the number of times Clara is heavier is $2020 \div 0.02$, which might be thought of as $2020 \div \frac{1}{50} = 2020 \times 50 = 101\,000$.

It is fun finding comparisons like the one here, and often the answers are surprising. You could compare the height of one of Britain's shortest mountains, Snaefell on the Isle of Man (621 m high), with that of Mount Everest (8848 m high). Or, maybe, compare the population density of London (12 000 people per sq. mile) with that of Greenland (15 sq. miles per person). How about the mass of an acorn (about 4 g) and the mass of a large oak tree (about 8 tonnes)? And don't forget the 220 km length of Britain's longest canal, the Grand Union Canal, set against the shortest, the Wardle Canal in Cheshire, which is a mere 47 m long!

Puzzling Problems – Answers and Notes

P62 D 16

A pattern of 18 tiles along and 14 tiles up, will require 3
complete rows of 4 patterns of 16 tiles (J) and 4 patterns of 8
tiles (K) as well as 3 patterns of 8 tiles (L) and 1 pattern of 4 tiles
(M):

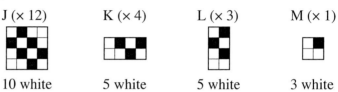

J (× 12)	K (× 4)	L (× 3)	M (× 1)
10 white	5 white	5 white	3 white

Therefore the number of white tiles will be
12 × 10 + 4 × 5 + 3 × 5 + 3 = 156 and so Tyler will need
to buy 160 tiles in 16 packs.

P63 C 384

The cubes painted on one face only are on the outside of the cube
but not at the edges or corners. Each of the six 10 by 10 faces
will have 8 × 8 such painted cubes, so the total number is
6 × 8 × 8 = 384.

P64 B 45°

I eat a quarter, leaving 270° of cake. This is divided into six
pieces, which have an angle of 270° ÷ 6 which is 45° for each
brother.

P65 B 2

If the median and mode are equal in a set of five numbers, then
at least three of the numbers are the same. In this case, these
three numbers are 4. As the range is 4, the smallest and largest
numbers must have a difference of 4. But a mean of 4 implies the
five numbers add up to 20. So the smallest and largest numbers
add up to 8 and have a difference of 4, and are therefore 2 and 6.

P66 B 14

90 is a multiple of 5, so the product of the remaining two
numbers is 18. They must therefore equal 3 and 6. So the sum is
3 + 5 + 6 = 14.
Try to investigate how the totals and products of three numbers
vary when three dice are thrown!

Puzzling Problems – Answers and Notes

P67 D $\dfrac{1}{2}$

This can be solved in at least two ways. Firstly, write down all the 36 combinations of possible numbers such as

1, 1	*1, 2*	1, 3	*1, 4*	1, 5	*1, 6*
2, *1*	2, 2	*2, 3*	2, 4	*2, 5*	2, 6
3, 1	etc				

Of these half have an even number and an odd number (in italic above).

P68 B 2

Because Dhiran's code is a multiple of 3, its digits must have a total that is a multiple of 3. The sum of 4, 5 and 1 is already 10, so the fourth digit could be 2, 5 or 8. Since 4515 is a multiple of 5 and 4518 is a multiple of 9, Dhiran's code is 4512.

P69 B $\dfrac{1}{3}$

Of the 18 chocolates there are $6 \times 2 = 12$ flavours that she likes. So the probability of Swee Tuth getting one she doesn't like is $\dfrac{6}{18} = \dfrac{1}{3}$.

P70 D **40%**

24 out of 60 boys choose pink for girls. That is 4 out of 10 and is 40%.

The numbers used in this problem are not from an actual survey but have been made up. But do your pupils think that young girl's bicycles must be pink? Or that their hobbies and interests must be very different to those of boys? How about a serious survey on this? The website www.pinkstinks.org.uk has some thoughts on the subject.

P71 A **black and orange (or orange and black)**

There is no scale on the vertical axis, but the frequencies of the colours are multiples of: red 3, orange 6, black 2, green 1 and yellow 4. The total is 16. The two colours which are the favourites of 50% of the class must add up to 8 and are black and orange.

Puzzling Problems – Answers and Notes

P72 E

According to Polly's observation, her graph should show children who do more sports to be good at football, and those who do less to be not so good, and with one exception. Graphs A and D show no connection (or correlation as mathematicians refer to it); graph B shows the very opposite of Polly's conclusion, and of graphs C and E, only E has an exception.

Very Challenging Problems – Answers and Notes

V1 B 654 ÷ (3 + 21)

A is 654 ÷ 33. B is 654 ÷ 24. C is 654 ÷ 33. D is 654 ÷ 31 and E is 654 ÷ 321. The value of a division sum is largest when the denominator is the smallest when the numerators are the same, so B is the answer.

V2 D 40p

All but 10 of the coins are 1p coins, which tells us that the number of 2p and 5p coins adds up to 10. Similarly, the total of the 1p and 5p coins is 10 and the total of the 1p and 2p coins is 10. He therefore has 5 of each coin, giving a total of $(5 \times 1) + (5 \times 2) + (5 \times 5) = 40$p.

V3 B 2

The second to last digit is always 2. For example 5^3 is 125. When multiplying this by 5, we see that it is inevitable that the second to last digit remains 2. Try repeated multiplication of 5 on a calculator.

V4 C 5

The first 9 numbers are single digits, so after writing these Kim has 91 digits left. Each number from 9 to 99 requires two digits, and so after writing 91 further digits Kim will have written another 45 (up to the number 54); the one digit left will be a 5.

V5 E 630 ml

Aunty needs $15 \times 3 \times 7 \times 2 = 630$ ml.

Very Challenging Problems – Answers and Notes

V6 A 5

There are 13 noses and so 13 'creatures'. The number of tails equals the number of dogs so pupils can use trial and error to find the answer. Or we can assume that each nose has 2 legs, giving us 26 legs and leaving 10 legs extra, suggesting 5 'things' which have 4 legs each, i.e. dogs.

Otherwise, using algebra, $p + d = 13$ and (for the legs) $2p + 4d = 36$. Subtracting twice the first from the second we get $2d = 10$ so $d = 5$.

How many tails would there be with the numbers of noses and legs shown below?

a) 15 noses and 50 legs → 10 tails

b) 8 noses and 24 legs → 4 tails

c) 8 noses and 16 legs → 0 tails

d) 8 noses and 32 legs → 8 tails

e) 10 noses and 8 legs → −6 tails.

Using algebra for the last question (p is the number of people and d is the number of dogs) gives: $p + d = 10$; $2p + 4d = 8$ → $p = 16$ and $d = -6$. The algebra allows us to enter a world with a negative number of dogs!

V7 E 4199

The final digit of the answer will be the same as the final digit to $3 \times 7 \times 9$ which is 9. So the four-digit number is 4199.

V8 E £1 990 000

$(5 \times £1000) + £5000 = £10\,000$. Now $£2\,000\,000 - £10\,000$ equals £1 990 000.

V9 D 6

The only square numbers with an odd number for the tens digit are 16 and 36. So Doris has six 1p coins.

V10 B 89p

It isn't necessary to calculate the price of each cake and doughnut. Subtracting the two 'sentences' tells us that three cakes and one doughnut will cost £2.06 − £1.17 = 89p. In fact, cakes cost 25p each and doughnuts cost 14p each.

V11 D 31

There are 10 seVens in the units digits, 10 seVentys, 9 fiVes in the units (as fifteen is not fiveteen) plus eleVen and twelVe.

If the question had asked how many Ls there were (instead of how many Vs) then the answer would have been two, with the third and fourth Ls not occurring until we reach 1 000 000.

V12 A 26

a must be 9 giving $7 \times 6 = 3$ carry 6.
Multiplying 7 by 6 adding the carried 6 gives 48 so $c = 4$. Write down the 0. 8×9 is 72 so $b = 8$. This gives $d = 5$. The total of these four numbers is $9 + 8 + 4 + 5 = 26$.

$$
\begin{array}{r}
6 \ a \\
\times \ b \ 7 \\
\hline
c \ 8 \ 3 \\
d \ 5 \ 2 \ 0 \\
\hline
6 \ 0 \ 0 \ 3
\end{array}
$$

V13 E impossible

12 miles at 6 mph takes two hours already, leaving no time in which to cover the remaining 12 miles. Therefore it is impossible!

Can children create other seemingly plausible (but actually impossible) problems? Can they explain why/where the 'impossibility' occurs?

V14 E 8

Pupils might start by choosing values for x and calculate how long Mr Urly worked. It turns out that whatever value is chosen for x, the answer is always 8. By algebra, we calculate that, in the morning he worked $12 - (x + 2) = 10 - x$ hours. In the afternoon he worked $x - 2$ hours. The total is $(10 - x) + (x - 2)$ and the xs cancel out to give 8 hours.

Very Challenging Problems – Answers and Notes

V15 D   56 cm²

The area of the octagon is the area of the square less the area of 4 corner triangles, so it is $8 \times 8 - 4 \times 2 = 56$ cm².

Using the same two 8 cm squares, the smallest area possible for the octagonal overlap is when the octagon is regular: the octagon then has an area of just over 53 cm². But another interesting question to ask is what other polygons can be made from the overlap of two identical squares? Some possibilities are shown below:

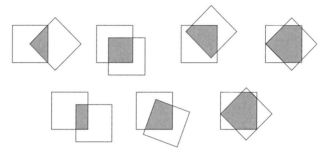

Can you find different polygons with the overlap if you allow the squares to be different sizes?

V16 E   75

40 teenage tadpoles weigh the same as 30 jolly jellyfish. Now $30 \div 2 = 15$, and so 30 jolly jellyfish weigh the same as $(15 \times 5) = 75$ nuclear newts.

V17 C   550 g

We can tell that one-third of the plum jam weighs $400 - 250 = 150$ g (without the pot itself). Hence the pot on its own weighs $250 - 150 = 100$ g, and a full pot of jam weighs $150 + 3 \times 150 = 550$ g.

V18 A   3 hours 30 minutes

If Anita can tidy 1 big and 3 small rooms in 90 minutes, she could manage 2 big and 6 small in $90 \times 2 = 180$ minutes. But 2 big rooms take her as long as 3 small rooms, so that she could tidy $3 + 6 = 9$ small rooms in 180 minutes. Thus one small room will take her $180 \div 9 = 20$ minutes, and so 3 big rooms and 6 small rooms will take her $3 \times 30 + 6 \times 20 = 210$ minutes $= 3$ hours and 30 minutes.

Very Challenging Problems – Answers and Notes

V19 E 11

The second-to-last sentence tells us that the number of cards is a square number; i.e. 9, 16, 25, 36, 49, 64, 81, 100, 121, 144, 169 or 196 (less than 200). The number we are looking for has to be one more than a multiple of 5, and so has its units digit one or six. It also has to have an odd units digit as it has 'one left over after being arranged in fours'. The number must end in one; i.e. it must be 81 or 121. Of these two, only 121 is one more than a multiple of six. So the number of cards on each side of the square is 11.

V20 C 1 : 4 : 15

Subtracting living costs gives the figures for other expenses as £4000, £16 000 and £60 000. These are in a ratio of 4 : 16 : 60. That is 1 : 4 : 15.

The gap between top and bottom earners in our country is still growing. Suppose the three people in this question were all given a 5% pay rise. How much increase in pay would they get? Can your pupils find a way of giving pay increases which *they* think is fair?

V21 D 56

There are only four positive cube numbers less than 100: 1, 8, 27 and 64. Lily is 64, Jilly is 27, Milly (the elder sister) is 8 and Tilly is 1. In this way, when Milly was born, Lily would have been 64 − 8 = 56 years old.

V22 E 12

It is probably easiest to try out each solution in turn.

V23 C 18.914

2% of 19.3 is (2 × 19.3) ÷ 100 = 38.6 ÷ 100 = 0.386. Usain Bolt's new time would therefore be 19.3 − 0.386 = 18.914.

V24 D 2160

In 30 hours the snail travels one mile. In this time the cheetah travels 72 × 30 = 2160 miles. So the cheetah is travelling 2160 times faster than the snail.

Very Challenging Problems – Answers and Notes

V25 B **18 seconds**

For every circuit that the faster car makes, see where the slower car lands up. After 9 seconds, the slower car has completed $\frac{3}{4}$ of a circuit; after 18 seconds, the slower car has completed $1\frac{1}{2}$ circuits and has now caught up with the faster car, so to speak. What if the two cars started at the same place, but went in opposite directions? When would they then meet?

V26 B **15**

If June 1st is a Monday, then the first Monday in July is July 6th, with the first Monday in August being August 3rd. The total of these dates is $1 + 6 + 3 = 10$. Trying each year in turn gives a highest total of 15.
What if the knitting club met on different days of the week? Does this make a difference?

V27 A **27.1**

At the end of the first year, 90% of the energy is used. At the end of the second year, 10% of 90 = 9, so 90% – 9% = 81%. 10% of 81 = 8.1, so 81% – 8.1% = 72.9%. The total reduction is therefore 100% – 72.9% = 27.1%.
For those children who are less secure with percentages, try starting with 1000 units of energy.

V28 D **1**

Adding the first three equations gives $a + b + c + d + e + f = 6$. Comparison with the fourth equation gives $a = 1$.

V29 C **4**

Knowing that $p = 3, q = 2$ and $p^3 \times q^2 \times r = 432$, we can replace the letters p and q for the numbers they represent. So $3^3 \times 2^2 \times r = 27 \times 4 \times r = 432$ and hence $r = 432 \div (27 \times 4) = 432 \div 108 = 4$.

V30 B **£10**

There are three winning scores greater than ten: 11, 11 and 12 (draw the 6 by 6 grid of outcomes when two dice are thrown). So, in 36 games, the player pays out £36 and receives £30, losing £6 on average. In 12 games she would therefore expect to lose £2. And in 60 games would therefore expect to lose £10.

Very Challenging Problems – Answers and Notes

Expectation is the topic here. It is the expected loss and may not be the actual loss. Some games have an expectation of zero – break even. Betting on heads of tails for a balanced die has a zero expectation. Can your pupils design any other games with zero expectation?

Some games such as slot machines have an expectation fixed by law. Others, such as roulette are fixed by their design. In these games there are many losers but some people manage to win. The National Lottery has a negative expectation, and most people lose. Why do some people think gambling is bad?

Expectation is a mathematical idea which has uses apart from gambling, and is an important topic in probability.

V31 D 24 weeks

There are 5 choices for who goes first in line, and after that 4 choices for who goes second, and then 3 for third, 2 for fourth and then 1 choice for who will have to be last: so $5 \times 4 \times 3 \times 2 \times 1 = 120$ ways. This means that they not have to repeat until after 120 days, or 24 school weeks.

This question involves a part of mathematics called permutations. Here 5 girls can be arranged in any order, and the number of different ways is $5 \times 4 \times 3 \times 2 \times 1 = 120$. This idea comes up so often that there is a short way of writing it using an exclamation mark! In this way $5! = 120$ (pronounced 'five factorial') – you may have a button on your calculator that will calculate these for you, though the numbers produced become very large very quickly. How many different ways are there of arranging all the letters of the word TRIANGLE into another 'word', even one that is not a word in any useful language?

V32 B 8

This problem is best worked out in rough…!

Children could make their own cards up and investigate how many such cards are needed to create different shapes.

V33 C 32

Dividing the square into quarters helps us see that exactly half the square is shaded. $8 \times 8 = 64$, and half of 64 is 32.

Very Challenging Problems – Answers and Notes

V34 B 20

The smoky bacon sector of the pie chart has an angle of 45°, and is one eighth of the full pie (360°). So the number of people in the survey must be divisible by eight. From the five numbers in the answers, only 20 is not divisible by eight.

Suppose that the smoky bacon angle had the exact angles below. What would be the *minimum* number of people in the surveys? 20°, 30°, 40°, 2°.

V35 B 4

Since we know where the 1 is placed, the possibilities for placing the number 2 are rather limited, so one approach is to explore where the 2 can be placed.

We shall refer to the circles as in the diagram below:

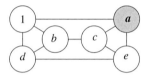

It is clear that 2 can be placed in either c or e, since a, b and d are joined to 1. If 2 is placed in c, then $d = 3, a = 4, b = 5$ and $e = 6$. Alternatively, if 2 is placed in e, then $b = 3, a = 4$, $e = 5$ and $d = 6$. In both cases, the number that is placed in circle a is 4.

V36 E orange

The diagrams show the position of the plates as they are moved according to the rules in the question.

Red	Green	Orange	Blue	Yellow	Red
Blue	Yellow	Red	Green	Orange	Blue
Green	Orange	Blue	Yellow	Red	Green
Yellow	Red	Green	Orange	Blue	Yellow
Orange	Blue	Yellow	Red	Green	Orange

Start.......... one move.... two moves.. three moves.. four moves...
beginning

The cycle returns to the initial position every five moves. So, after twenty one moves the middle plate will be orange.

Pupils could work out what the centre plate would be after 101

76

similar changes. They could look at the rules for using four plates, six plates (maybe examining the bottom plate in each of these as there will be no middle plate). Is there a general rule? If we had just three plates (red, blue, green) what would be the middle plate after 1000 moves? (red)

There are many other cyclic situations to examine; days of the week, hours on a clock, unit digits when counting, units digits in the times tables and traffic lights.

V37 B 96

Going from left to right from one house to the next, the house numbers on the top row increase by one, but the house numbers on the bottom row decrease by one each time. This means that the total of the numbers of houses opposite each other remains the same for each pair of facing houses. For the pair of houses we know about this total is $46 + 145 = 191$, but we also know that the shaded house and the house facing it have consecutive numbers. Therefore they must be numbered $(191 - 1) \div 2$ and $(191 + 1) \div 2$, that is, 95 and 96.

The idea of totals remaining the same is a very useful notion – it occurs in the famous story of the mathematician Gauss (1777-1855), who in school was asked by his frustrated teacher to work out

$$1 + 2 + 3 + 4 + \ldots + 97 + 98 + 99 + 100.$$

Gauss did so by noticing that $1 + 100 = 101, 2 + 99 = 101, 3 + 98 = 101$, and so on, hence making the calculation equivalent to the sum of 50 pairs of numbers with a sum of 101, that is $50 \times 101 = 5050$. It also has interesting consequences in the numbering of the pages of newspapers, where a single folded sheet of paper has two printed pages on each side. It can be seen that, like this, the two page numbers on each side will have the same total for every side of every sheet. On one side of one of the inside sheets of my newspaper today the page numbers are as shown below:

Can you tell from this how many pages there are altogether, and how many sheets of paper are needed for the whole newspaper?

The Primary Mathematics Challenge

The problems in this book are taken from the Primary Mathematics Challenge (PMC) papers from November 2010 to February 2014. In the November PMC papers, the last five questions have no suggested answers – we have added five multiple choice answers in this book.

The PMC is aimed at school pupils aged 11 or less. In September and October, schools order packs of ten challenge papers (which include Answers and Notes and certificates for everyone). Pupils take the challenge in a given week in November. The top scoring pupils are then invited to take the PMC Bonus Round in the following February. Questions from these are also included in this book. For further information, visit the PMC pages at www.primarymathschallenge.org.uk. The problems set in the PMC Bonus Round are very difficult for primary-aged pupils, and therefore will also challenge younger secondary pupils.

Copyright Statement

Thanks

Lots of teachers have been members of the PMC Problems Team over the years and have prepared the PMC papers over the years. Thanks go to Colin Abell, Peter Bailey, Sue Barber, Chris Eva, Lesley Jones, Tania Kimberley, Rudolf Loewenstein, Katherine Milner, Robyn Pickles, John Place, Joseph Tazzyman, Alex Voice and Brian Weller. Thank you to Robyn for problem selection, and to Peter and Lesley for checking through the drafts. Thanks also to Alex Voice for formatting the papers and to Bill Richardson for his work in formatting this book.

Challenge your pupils 3:
using problem-solving questions from the Primary Mathematics Challenge

This book contains over 200 multiple choice problems which aim to interest and motivate pupils. They cover a full range of mathematics topics and are provided with answers, notes and follow-up ideas. The problems can be used by both primary (and secondary) teachers in class, for homework, and maths clubs.

The problems are taken from the Primary Mathematics Challenge papers from 2010 to 2014. They are presented in four categories – Easy, Harder, Puzzling and Very Challenging. Most pupils between the ages of 9 and 14 should be able to answer the problems in the Easy and Harder sections, but many problems in the Puzzling and Very Challenging sections will challenge the brightest pupils in both primary and secondary schools.

ISBN 978-0-906588-87-1
© 2016 the Mathematical Association

PUBLISHED BY

The Mathematical Association
259 London Road
Leicester
LE2 3BE
Tel: 0116 221 0013
Fax: 0116 212 2835
Email: office@m-a.org.uk

www.m-a.org.uk

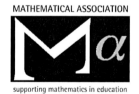

MATHEMATICAL ASSOCIATION

supporting mathematics in education